The Comic Spirit of Wallace Stevens

The *Comic Spirit of Wallace Stevens*
Daniel Fuchs

Duke University Press, Durham, N. C., 1963

To my parents and Cara

This book is published with the assistance
of funds from a grant to the Duke University Press
by the Ford Foundation

This is an interpretive study and, to a lesser extent, an evaluation. My method is exegesis, with the exception of the first chapter which is mainly cultural history. This is not a study of the poet as a craftsman but as a mind, and as a performer on a cultural stage. A thorough analysis of his formal accomplishments and his debt to specific poets would be a subject for another book, a needed book. I have proceeded thematically rather than chronologically, since the problems in Stevens criticism now are, to my mind, likely to concern what he is saying rather than how he has developed or changed. This approach is especially germane to Stevens since he is not only a difficult poet but a poet who does not have very different phases, as does Yeats. He does, of course, change, but his changes are different ways of exploring the same themes, themes which are sufficiently complex to justify a lifetime's meditation. Though they are all present in *Harmonium*, these themes achieve expression, some of them fullest expression, well after *Harmonium*. Yet it is significant that Stevens contemplated calling his volume of collected poems *The Whole of Harmonium*.

As the title indicates, I have approached Stevens through his comic sense. This is not a peripheral approach. His comic spirit is central, and without a sense of it, there is no true understanding of Stevens. Most of his comic poems are discussed. Since comedy is ultimately a serious business, some of the poems discussed are not funny at all, but essential in explaining the beliefs and prejudices which constitute what I will show to be a typically modern comic sense.

I am grateful for this opportunity to thank the late Richard Chase and Samuel French Morse for their valuable criticisms and encouragement. Also, an interview with Mr. Morse at South Hadley supplied me with some little known facts about Stevens. I wish to thank William York Tindall for a close, enthusiastic reading of the manuscript and a footnote on Apollinaire. Thanks go to J. V. Ridgely and Isadore Traschen for their close reading of the manuscript. I also wish to thank Irving Howe, whose admiration for Stevens' poetry proved contagious. Finally, for permission to quote from Stevens' letters to Ronald Lane Latimer and Hi Simons I wish to thank Mr. Morse and Robert Rosenthal of Special Collections at the University of Chicago Library.

All poems quoted are to be found in *The Collected Poems of Wallace Stevens* (which is indexed), with the exception of those found in *Opus Posthumous*, in which case I have used the letters *(OP)* in the text as an indication.

Contents

The Comic Spirit of Wallace Stevens

Chapter 1: Stevens' Comic Milieu

*R*eading Stevens poses an immediate problem. The reader is dazzled by a display of
verbal pyrotechnics, a shower of exotic colors, wondrous sound-effects,
inkhorn words, hoo-hoos and rum-tum-tums, euphonious geography,
exquisite insults. The reader may very well not survive his bedazzle-
ment. Or, if he is spirited enough to indulge his imagination and see
what it is that Stevens is doing, Stevens' ideas may prove to be even
more disquieting than his formidable means of expressing them, and
the poet go unread on that account. Stevens dares you to read him,
and there was a time when few accepted the challenge. His brilliant
first volume, *Harmonium*, published when he was forty-four years old,
did not make nearly the stir in 1923 that it has been making since
then. Ornate, bizarre, difficult, and middle-aged, it succeeded perhaps
too well in dismaying the reader. It is the work of neither a young

poet nor a traditional poet, nor, to the reader of 1923, was it the work of a well-known modern. Its unaccommodating surface is further complicated by an oblique and various presentation of the poet's voice. Its youthfulness, and there is much of the stylish twenties youthfulness in it, is calculated. Yet its extreme comic sophistication is something of an affectation, an affectation by virtue of which Stevens may say what is genuine. Stevens affects the dandy. That is, he is an American dandy which, in our time, is a contradiction in terms. Nevertheless, this is the first mask the reader of Stevens must contend with, the first of several comic masks which he uses as façades to hide profound yet sometimes playful feelings, and as hyperbolic means of expression.

Dandyism cannot exist in twentieth-century America, except by insinuation. What kind of dandy is it who would come to terms with gray flannel suits, sincere neckties, and insurance litigation? What dandy could exist in this energetic world of organized, common affairs? Not that he would lack the necessary *ennui*. But he could not summon up the hypercivilized manners of an aristocracy — of wealth or of intellect — which cultivates its graces with excessive assiduousness and display because it knows it is waning. Manners in the sense of deliberate social hauteur are, in our democracy, considered an object of ridicule rather than a sign of distinction. Even if he had the desire, Stevens could not shine where the dandy must — the public theater, the *beau monde* which the dandy considers a stage made for him to act upon. But Stevens was far from having this desire. His public self was notoriously unobtrusive, if indeed, he can be said to have had a public self at all in the sense that a poet may. "No American we have ever published has been so retiring or has let us see so little of him," writes Alfred Knopf.[1] Alfred Kreymborg too comments, perhaps with some exaggeration, about Stevens' curious reticence, about the Stevens who waves a deprecating hand and utters something that sounds like "Jesus" when cornered about his own poetry, about the Stevens who gives Kreymborg the manuscript of "Peter Quince at the Clavier" with the hasty proviso — "I must ask you not to breathe a word about this. Print it if you like; send it back if you don't."[2] Far from being an exhibitionistic, exotic flower in the

1. Alfred Knopf, statement about Stevens in Stevens issue, *Trinity Review*, VIII (May, 1954), 32.
2. Alfred Kreymborg, *Troubadour* (New York: Sagamore Press, 1957), pp. 170, 187.

quotidian desert, Stevens, it is now and then reported, kept his poetic identity something of a secret. "We don't talk about poetry here," Stevens told Samuel French Morse at the posh Hartford Canoe Club.[3] William York Tindall tells of his meeting a fellow insurance executive of Stevens', who worked for the Hartford Accident and Indemnity Company. He had corresponded with Stevens and when Tindall half-jokingly suggested that the letters were valuable, he incredulously replied, "Wally's letters valuable?" Tindall said that Stevens was an important man. The executive said, "Wally, important?" Tindall said that he was a wonderful poet. The executive said, "Wally! Poetry?"[4]

Yes, Wally poetry. Not only poetry but poems, as we might expect, about the act of writing poetry and the meaning of this act, about the enormous pressure exerted against the imagination by social reality, about integrations of imagination and fact which are not ridiculous. It is a poetry full of travesty and self-irony, the dandiacal import of which may be more clearly understood if we refer, very briefly, to a period of poetry which influenced it — French poetry of the 1860's and thereafter.

Baudelaire is the key figure here and Laforgue pointed to his underlying importance when he said that he was the first to break with the public,[5] its taste as well as its morality. Baudelaire, Laforgue, and the symbolists engage in a combat against the old rhetoric and in so doing against the class which hid behind it. Psychologically depressing to the poet, this proved culturally advantageous. The disdain of the poet was fed. "One even comes to wonder," writes Roger Shattuck, "if the modernist movement would ever have taken shape without the academics, the philistines, and the entrenched bourgeoisie of Paris."[6] Satire and irony, rage and obscurity replaced the simple lyric tone of Hugo and Musset, as dandyism found a stage in literature as well as in manners. If old feelings were sacrificed, new, more complicated, more self-conscious and more enlarged feelings were born, as were various odd and esoteric ways of expressing them. Baudelaire

3. Interview with Samuel French Morse, March 15, 1960. All subsequent citations of Morse refer to this interview.
4. Interview with William York Tindall, October, 1959.
5. Jules Laforgue, *Selected Writings of Jules Laforgue*, edited and translated by William Jay Smith (New York: Grove Press, 1956), p. 213.
6. Roger Shattuck, "How Poetry Got Its Teeth: Paris, 1857 and After," *Western Review*, XXIII (Winter, 1959), 117.

represented a gain in passion, Laforgue a gain in detachment. It was for the artistically conservative French to make the first modernist statement of what we still consider contemporary literature, at least in the academic sense. Poetry was saved from the poetic. "Dandysme," Shattuck writes, "or clenched Romanticism replaced the lyric tone." An "icy and elegant manner barely revealed the flame within," as conventionalized emotion was replaced by "a calculus of feeling."[7] Both artist and dandy, or the artist as dandy, found pleasure in distinguishing himself from the herd. Baudelaire's habitual black attire was fashionable because it was unfashionable, because it was unique. He also shocked conventional taste when he said, in his art criticism,[8] that nature lacked imagination in not making meadows red and trees blue. Laforgue too expressed an identity between dandyism and his art when, in opposition to conventional formalism, he said that genius consisted in being unique and could point to the tone and metrics of his own verse as an example. And Baudelaire's adherence to formal convention served to add a shock of unexpectedness to what he had to say. As he writes in the section on the dandy in "The Painter of Modern Life," dandyism "is above all a burning need to acquire originality, within the apparent bounds of convention. It is a sort of cult of oneself, which can dispense even with what are commonly called illusions. It is the delight in causing astonishment, and the proud satisfaction of never oneself being astonished .... Dandyism is the last gleam of heroism in times of decadence."[9] Above all a dandy in his poetry, Baudelaire gave his poems the meticulous attention that the Regency dandy gave to his appearance.

Although Wallace Stevens' dandyism is more muted, wry, and less intense than Baudelaire's — even Baudelaire's dandyism did not measure up to all of his utterances about it — it does share the qualities of deflationary assault, disillusion, icy elegance, oddity, uniqueness, self-conscious absorption, the desire to astonish, and a new, complex, and in some sense bizarre means of expression. Although this last quality is not constant in Stevens — he often writes in a plain discursive

7. *Ibid.*, XXIII, 179.
8. See Enid Starkie, *Baudelaire* (London: Faber and Faber, 1957), p. 294. Charles Baudelaire, "The Salon of 1859," *The Mirror of Art*, edited and translated by Jonathan Mayne (New York: Doubleday Anchor Books, 1956), pp. 233 f., 238, 240.
9. Charles Baudelaire, "The Painter of Modern Life," *The Essence of Laughter and Other Essays, Journals and Letters*, edited by Peter Quennel, translated by Norman Cameron (New York: Meridian Books, 1956), pp. 48 f.

style, and esteems nature as highly as he esteems artifice — he sometimes gives the impression, to paraphrase d'Aurevilly, that he lives on his Alexandrine uniqueness as on a bed of spikes.

If, like Baudelaire, Stevens feels a sense of dislocation between the imaginative man and social reality, he too benefited from the existence of stale taste. His wit thrives on the deflation of conventional ways of feeling and writing when the convention has little to do with the way things are. Like the outcast of poverty, the outcast of imagination found that there was a certain luck in being very unlucky. His alienation had the great advantage of enabling him to define clearly the things he really cared about, and reject definitely that about which he cared nothing at all. Again Stevens' alienation is not so dramatic or so encompassing as Baudelaire's, and not so pathetic as Laforgue's, but it is there as an abiding presence in his poetry, enriching both his scorn for the general American lack of refinement and his self-ironic uneasiness at being that somewhat superfluous contemporary figure, the poet.

This combination of antagonism and disillusion may take the form of a longing for *dix-huitième* elegance in Stevens, a taste probably acquired from Verlaine. The poem called "The Weeping Burgher" is a case in point. Weeping burgher like American dandy seems to be a contradiction in terms, since the burgher (the somewhat refined word itself is a contradiction of solid middle-class citizenry) is happily absorbed in the world of getting and spending, and has hardly any cause for weeping about his secure social status. Yet, Stevens' persona here is a weeping burgher, an alienated, arty burgher who denies his position in favor of a sense of taste which he feels is aristocratic and, he knows, ridiculous for being so.

> It is with a strange malice
> That I distort the world.
>
> Ah! that ill humors
> Should mask as white girls.
> And ah! that Scaramouche
> Should have a black barouche.
>
> The sorry verities!
> Yet in excess, continual,
> There is cure of sorrow.

His malice is strange in that it is the expression of taste, which is an oddity in a world of burghers. Seeing nothing but "sorry verities" in the mundane world about him, he longs for a past which had wit, buffoonery, romance — and the words "Scaramouche" and "barouche" — to recommend it. The mere fact that the burgher desires elegance and manners makes his position extreme. Style, in his circumstances, is something which is by definition excessive. Yet his dandyism is homeopathic. This excess called style is that which reconciles him, in an attenuated way, to the middle-class sameness. His malice is not militant. It is tempered by the self-irony of a man who recognizes the old age of his desire.

> Permit that if as ghost I come
> Among the people burning in me still,
> I come as belle design
> Of foppish line.
>
> And I, then, tortured for old speech,
> A white of wildly woven rings;
> I, weeping in a calcined heart,
> My hands such sharp, imagined things.

A ghost because he lives in a rather distant past, he apologizes for his taste for a lost elegance with Prufrockish self-denial. Prufrock too saw himself as a dandy in a self-ironic way.

> Shall I part my hair behind? Do I dare to
>   eat a peach?
> I shall wear white flannel trousers, and walk
>   upon the beach.

Like Prufrock the weeping burgher feels superfluous and foppish. Like Prufrock he is

> Full of high sentence, but a bit obtuse;
> At times, indeed, almost ridiculous —
> Almost, at times, the Fool.

The word "calcined," which means both desiccated and purified by consuming the grosser part, seems to indicate the double feeling which Stevens has for his burgher. It is one of those inkhorn words which, as R. P. Blackmur has shown,[10] Stevens chooses with precise knowledge. For the burgher is admirable insofar as he does indeed pursue his quest for elegance in an inelegant time and place; he is purified by his purgation of the gross. But he is also devastated in that the gap between verity and his desire is ludicrously great. This vast difference is underscored by the concluding image. Unlike the smiling burgher who has common, useful hands, the weeping burgher sees even his hands as a subject for his aristocratic imagination. They are, perhaps, useless, but especially vivid for being merely gentlemanly. He is indeed refined, but like Prufrock, refined perhaps beyond the point of civilization.

The victories of taste, however, are not always so costly. The dandy's rich contempt is not always mixed with self-irony. When his exquisite taste is lavished on something as mundane as bananas, it is done in a way which transforms the ordinary, as in "Floral Decorations for Bananas."

> Well, nuncle, this plainly won't do.
> These insolent, linear peels
> And sullen, hurricane shapes
> Won't do with your eglantine.
> They require something serpentine.
> Blunt yellow in such a room!
>
> You should have had plums tonight,
> In an eighteenth-century dish,
> And pettifogging buds,
> For the women of primrose and purl,
> Each one in her decent curl.
> Good God! What a precious light!

Again a fanciful dandiacal figure projects an identity between taste and the *dix-huitième*. We are concerned in this poem, a typical dandiacal concern, with a matter of dress. Proper attire, that is properly dazzling, is so much an understood matter in the dandy's world that even bananas have apposite dress. Without it they are arrant commoners — insolent, sullen, ignobly shaped, blunt — an insult to the elegantly coifed women. The exclamation with which the second

10. R. P. Blackmur, *Form and Value in Modern Poetry* (New York: Doubleday Anchor Books, 1957), pp. 185 ff.

stanza concludes — "Good God! What a precious light!" — may be Stevens commenting on the icy showiness of the first two stanzas, just as it is his persona's comment on the exquisite appearance of the excessively refined women. Similarly, the bananas may be considered the inelegance of the contemporary scene.

> But bananas hacked and hunched . . .
> The table was set by an ogre,
> His eye on an outdoor gloom
> And a stiff and noxious place.

Yet, to the dandy, bananas too have their refinement, just as the mundane may be enhanced by clothing itself in imagination. The women, of course, will dress to fit the occasion.

> Pile the bananas on planks.
> The women will be all shanks
> And bangles and slatted eyes.

> And deck the bananas in leaves
> Plucked from the Carib trees,
> Fibrous and dangling down,
> Oozing cantankerous gum
> Out of their purple maws,
> Darting out of their purple craws
> Their musky and tingling tongues.

In this jungle it is survival of the well-fitted.

Stevens' propensity for the exquisite issues into some of the gaudiest insults on record. No poet has used colors so successfully as a figure denoting the colorlessness of the plain, domestic scene. Witness the superfine barbarism of "Exposition of the Contents of a Cab" (*OP*).

> Victoria Clementina, negress,
> Took seven white dogs
> To ride in a cab.

> Bells of the dogs chinked.
> Harness of the horses shuffled
> Like brazen shells.

Oh-hé-hé! Fragrant puppets
By the green lake-pallors,
She too is flesh,

And a breech-cloth might wear,
Netted of topaz and ruby
And savage blooms;

Thridding the squawkiest jungle
In a golden sedan
White dogs at bay.

What breech-cloth might you wear —
Except linen, embroidered
By elderly women?

Opposed to the exotic negress are those figures of domestic paleness, who, in their lack of liveliness, seem mere puppets rather than vivid people. Imaginative intransigence here, as elsewhere in Stevens, is informed by a tone of exaggerated playfulness, not unlike that of the nineteenth-century French dandy who walked a lobster on a leash. Stevens holds the all too dun up to the scrutiny of the only too brilliant, two worlds in hyperbolic conflict in the mind of the conformist-dandy.

These dandiacal poems, written largely in the late teens and early twenties, are something of a joke — not merely the kind of joke about a black woman with seven white dogs. Stevens is not only manufacturing astonishment, he is having a good time in doing so. He is sharing in the postwar gaiety which is perhaps most associated in America with James Branch Cabell. Afred Kazin, writing about "The Pagan Exquisites," describes well this cultural euphoria of the older, unlost generation:

[a] superior elect...felt only they were living in a perpetual spirit of holiday....
Old barriers were down, down forever. American writers had proclaimed their official emancipation and their entry into the charmed halls of international civilization .... They wanted to prove ... that Americans too — especially Americans — could write richly and wickedly and idly. They fought no battles save the great battle of the twenties against Puritanism, against Mencken's great American Boob.[11]

11. Alfred Kazin, *On Native Grounds* (New York: Harcourt, Brace, 1942), pp. 227 f., 230.

Stevens shares in the windfall. His tasteful poetry is, by conventional standards of art and morality, in bad taste. Here again he is indulging in one of the pleasures of the dandy, the pleasure which Baudelaire describes when he says, "The intoxicating thing about bad taste is the aristocratic pleasure in giving offense."[12] Baudelaire's conception of the dandy comes closest to Stevens' when it is relaxed. Stevens is in sympathy with Baudelaire when the latter says, "Dandyism: What is the superior man? One who is not a specialist. The man of leisure and broad education. The rich man who loves work."[13] But Baudelaire's more violent statements about the dandy's personal detachment and superiority (even over the poet) are foreign to Stevens, whose desire for a tense originality is often hard to distinguish from his desire for a relaxed one. Stevens' desire for originality expresses itself as gaiety rather than asceticism. He was a dandy above all in his poetry, and though he carried his high value upon taste into his private life, his public life seemed an anti-self. Commenting on Stevens' dandyism, his friend William Carlos Williams writes, "He was a dandy at heart. You never saw Stevens in sloppy clothes. His poems are the result."[14] Although Stevens was no Beau Brummell, he was, it seems, one of the best dressed men in the insurance company, or at least, the only famous poet in America who could afford, and would wear, expensive suits and neckties. Williams recalls that Stevens had "a stage when [he] was fascinated to receive from a friend a box of joujous fresh from Paris. Help yourself. Candied violet petals! You'd be surprised at the kick I get out of such things."[15] Surprised? Is this not the kind of eccentricity we might expect from a dandy? Not from an American dandy. Even this modest exhibitionism concerns private taste rather than a public image. If the dandyism of a Brummell was a struggle between manners and boredom, Stevens' dandyism is a struggle between reality and boredom. Stevens is a dandy of the imagination as Brummell was of society. Both share a climate of hypercivility, eccentricity, overbreeding, haughty wit, apparent dispassionateness — but Stevens' dandyism lies essentially in poems, Brummell's in gestures.

12. Baudelaire, "Rockets," *The Essence of Laughter* . . . , p. 170.
13. Baudelaire, "My Heart Laid Bare," *The Essence of Laughter* . . . , p. 184.
14. William Carlos Williams, "Wallace Stevens," *Poetry*, LXXXVII (Jan., 1956), 236.
15. Williams, *Poetry*, p. 234.

At its least self-conscious, Stevens' dandyism reduces itself to hedonism, Fat Jocundus (as he calls himself in "The Glass of Water") as the nomad exquisite (as he is in "Nomad Exquisite"), the reflective poet as tourist. Lionel Abel acutely observes that the occasion for this poetry is the moment of moral release from the obligation of work, but goes awry in treating Stevens as a holiday poet alone.[16] Too much has been made of this aspect of his poetry since Yvor Winters' misleading essay.[17] Indeed, some of the poems which appear to be strictly travel-book pictures are subtle statements about the nature of the imagination. The poem which is often taken as the archetype of this poetry, "Nomad Exquisite," is itself a case in point.

> As the immense dew of Florida
> Brings forth
> The big-finned palm
> And green vine angering for life,
>
> As the immense dew of Florida
> Brings forth hymn and hymn
> From the beholder,
> Beholding all these green sides
> And gold sides of green sides,
>
> And blessed mornings,
> Meet for the eye of the young alligator,
> And lightning colors
> So, in me, come flinging
> Forms, flames, and the flakes of flames.

For all its lush scenery and hedonist celebration, for all its lightness, "Nomad Exquisite" is, like Wordsworth's "Tintern Abbey," a poem about the relation between nature and the perceiver, in which the creative power of nature ignites the creative power of the perceiver. Similarly, "Fabliau of Florida," while it is a beautiful tableau of beach and stars, is also about the endless integrations of imagination and reality.

16. Lionel Abel, "In the Sacred Park," *Partisan Review*, XXV (Winter, 1958), 86-98.
17. Yvor Winters, "Wallace Stevens, or the Hedonist's Progress," *In Defense of Reason* (Denver: University of Denver Press, 1943), pp. 431-459.

> Barque of phosphor
> On the palmy beach,
>
> Move outward into heaven,
> Into the alabasters
> And night blues.
>
> Foam and cloud are one,
> Sultry moon-monsters
> Are dissolving.
>
> Fill your black hull
> With white moonlight.
>
> There will never be an end
> To this droning of the surf.

Also, "Sea Surface Full of Clouds," a dandy's tour de force, is an implicit statement about the Protean force of the imagination adequate to the Protean force of nature. His "November of Tehuantepec" is not, as some critics have seen it, remote or irresponsible. Even the jokes within the poems themselves should be understood as an indispensable part of the dandy's holiday, as in the line from "Sea Surface" —

> The conch
> Of loyal conjuration trumped.

With all the sophisticated imaginative jugglery of this poem, it is fitting that the day makes its final appearance as a "Good clown."

Stevens may even be intimidated by his excessive refinement. He may even check his flair for the dazzling word in mid-air, but his delight in the odd word for its own sake wins out.

> The grackles sing avant the spring
> Most spiss — oh! Yes, most spissantly.
> They sing right puissantly.

> ("Snow and Stars")

And there are times, in his early poetry, when this flair for the dazzling surface is the only motivation of the poem. At these times Stevens gives the impression that one must be high to experience high culture, as in "Lulu Gay" (OP).

> She made the eunuchs ululate . . .
> "Olu" the eunuchs cried. "Ululalu."

Or in this excerpt from "Stanzas for 'Le Monocle de Mon Oncle' "
(OP), where alliteration is used for comic, dandified effect.

> Poets of pimpernel, unlucky pimps
> Of pomp, in love and good ensample, see
> How I exhort her, huckstering my woe.
> *"Oh, hideous, horrible, horrendous hocks!"* . . .
> *"Oh, lissomeness turned lagging ligaments!"*

This overdressed verse is part of the perpetual spirit of holiday which
Kazin refers to. Fortunately, it is not a spirit perpetually present in
Stevens. Although neither of the last two poems is included by
Stevens in the edition of his collected poems, both are symptomatic
of the excessive refinement which informs a good part of *Harmonium*,
and some of the poetry written after it. When, in "Le Monocle de
Mon Oncle," one reads

> Last night, we sat beside a pool of pink,
> Clippered with lilies scudding the bright chromes,
> Keen to the point of starlight, while a frog
> Boomed from his very belly odious chords

one feels that he has reached a new stage in American refinement,
which is self-ironic for being so refined.

Stevens, Cabell, Carl Van Vechten (who, according to Kreymborg,
persuaded Alfred Knopf to publish *Harmonium*), Elinor Wylie,
Donald Evans, and, in a different way, H. L. Mencken were writers
who sought the antidote of taste for the malady of the land of George
F. Babbitt. The link between spirits as disparate as Cabell and
Mencken — in addition to Mencken's excessive praise of Cabell — is
art. Both tried to vivify the American cultural scene by establishing
the reality of a native culture which was on a par with the European.
A book like *Jurgen* could be so extravagantly praised only in a culture
in which imagination was conspicuously lacking. If not *Jurgen*, then
Babbitt. But the refinement of *Jurgen, Jennifer Lorn, Peter Whiffle*,
seems now, and has seemed since the thirties, beside the point. These
books live so much for the refinement of life that most of life is

excluded from them. Mencken shared with Cabell and Stevens jokes about Puritanism, God, public morality, American drabness. But if Mencken and Stevens, in their very different ways, were men of art, only Stevens was the man of refined taste.

That which distinguishes Stevens from the aforementioned pagan exquisite spirit is the direction of his seriousness, the fact that one is witnessing an involvement with contemporary life which extends well beyond the *livresque*. His insight into the gains and losses of the imaginative man in our society, his sustained attempt at the promulgation of a new fiction in the face of the breakdown of belief, his awareness of the personal disorder of our time testify to the ultimacy of this seriousness. An astonishing stylist, he is yet so much more than a fine writer. In Stevens the experience of imagining receives articulate and deeply reflective expression. If the checkered career of the imagination in America has forced Stevens into half-ironic, half-scornful guises like the dandy, it also makes for another of his masks, one concerning the untrammeled feeling of imaginative power, a mask which might be called the poet as powerhouse.

The poetry after *Harmonium* is, generally speaking, written in a style less gaudy and bizarre. Stevens says farewell to holiday Florida, and Tehuantepec is likely to be replaced in the poet's meditations by the local landscapes of Jersey City, New Haven, or Hartford. The thirties, with hard economic times and political turmoil culminating in Hitler, swept the gilt carpet from under the feet of the pagan exquisites. Yet Stevens, who shared their pursuit of pleasure, their celebration of the graceful, their irreverent laughter, had much more than these qualities to recommend him, though in him these were a considerable recommendation in themselves. The violence of social and political reality strengthened his sense of the necessity of poetry, the necessity of propounding a new fiction. For him poetry emerged as the strongest force in the world, capable of constructing reality anew just as it is capable of destroying fictions which appear obsolete. As it destroys the old it presents the new with an enormous strength, substituting the power of possession for the misery of loss.

> That's what misery is,
> Nothing to have at heart.
> It is to have or nothing.

It is a thing to have,
A lion, an ox in his breast,
To feel it breathing there.

Corazon, stout dog,
Young ox, bow-legged bear,
He tastes its blood, not spit.

He is like a man
In the body of a violent beast.
Its muscles are his own . . .

The lion sleeps in the sun.
Its nose is on its paws.
It can kill a man.

("Poetry Is a Destructive Force")

Stevens feels so strongly the power of his imaginative integrations
that he sees them as figures of superhuman strength, sees them, perhaps, as circus animals which do not desert. This tremendous inner
violence of the imagination is what can be fatal to the meaningless-
ness prevailing outside the poet's self. The dandiacal surface is not
present. There is neither ridicule nor self-irony. Yet a comic effect is
achieved through the language of what might be called the carnival
of the imagination, a dreamlike sense of well-being derived from the
inner power of poetry. The poem is similar in wit and thoughtful high
spirits to "The Latest Freed Man," where the hero has destroyed the
old rhetoric and is transformed "From a doctor into an ox." The
wrong descriptions of the world, no less than the lack of any description at all, are part of the imaginative chaos which the modern poet
must master. The poet must be a lion since the challenges he meets
in his attempts to understand and master the natural world are themselves seen by Stevens to be monstrous. He writes in "The Man with
the Blue Guitar":

That I may reduce the monster to
Myself, and then may be myself

In the face of the monster, be more than part
Of it, more than the monstrous player of

One of its monstrous lutes, not be
Alone, but reduce the monster and be,

Two things, the two together as one,
And play of the monster and of myself,

Or better not of myself at all,
But of that as its intelligence,

Being the lion in the lute
Before the lion locked in stone.

We are fortunate in having Stevens' gloss on this passage, in which he asserts his imaginative imperialism, the imagination as lion.

> I want, as a poet, to be that in nature which constitutes nature's very self. I want to be nature in the form of a man, with all the resources of nature: I want to be the lion in the lute; and then, when I am, I want to face my parent and be his true poet. I want to face nature the way two lions face one another — the lion in the lute facing the lion locked in stone. I want as a man of the imagination, to write poetry with all the power of a monster equal in strength to that of the monster about whom I wrote. I want man's imagination to be completely adequate in the face of reality.[18]

If utterances like these are far from the dandy and his *beau monde* in style, they are not far from him in intention. Both seek a daring transformation of what Stevens likes to call the quotidian, the imposing mediocrity which challenges his claim to power and selfhood.

Related even more closely to the powerhouse mask is the mask of the metaphysician. If Stevens is going to proclaim the power of poetry to a hall which is not empty, he must make clear the nature of the reality he wishes to exalt. It does not take us long to find out that Stevens' metaphysicians are poets dabbling skilfully in metaphysics. He is not a poet who would pay philosophy the compliment of being systematically metaphysical. Whereas his poetic personae take on superhuman strength, his metaphysicians are likely to be a little laughable, mock-philosophical, pompously academic, tired, confused, stuck. Whether they are reading "Extracts from Addresses to the Academy of Fine Ideas" or an "Academic Discourse at Havana," Stevens' metaphysicians, epistemologists, scholars, and rabbis labor under the distinct disadvantage of being observed by a poet who perversely implies

18. Wallace Stevens, *Mattino Domenicale ed altre poesie*, edited and translated by Renato Poggioli (Turino: Giulio Einaudi, 1953), p. 179.

that metaphysics as well as poetry is the province of the poet. For example, in the poem mischievously called "Theory," Stevens treats the nature of the self as an aesthetic problem.

> I am what is around me.
>
> Women understand this.
> One is not duchess
> A hundred yards from a carriage.
>
> These, then are portraits:
> A black vestibule;
> A high bed sheltered by curtains.
>
> These are merely instances.

"Merely instances" is most of what the poet has to offer, instances that convince. The magic of ordinary experience is the poet's logic.

Similarly, the drifting of curtains in the poem "The Curtains in the House of the Metaphysician" is perceived in a surprisingly non-metaphysical manner. Its essence is not conceptually derived but perceived by analogy. Indeed, it is the manner of simile, the poet's device.

> It comes about that the drifting of these
>   curtains
> Is full of long motions; as the ponderous
> Deflations of distance; or as clouds
> Inseparable from their afternoons;
> Or the changing of light, the dropping
> Of the silence, wide sleep and solitude
> Of night, in which all motion
> Is beyond us, as the firmament,
> Up-rising and down-falling, bares
> The last largeness, bold to see.

Despite the philosophical "it comes about," and the many phrases in Stevens' poetry like it in tone, Stevens' intention is clear. By using the nominal trappings and by imitating the methods of the philosopher, Stevens is claiming for poetry the province usually claimed by philosophy, the definition of truth. Not that poetry has not often claimed its priority on truth. But the pseudo-speculation and pseudo-analysis which Stevens likes to dramatize are not usually associated with poetry. In our time, the promulgation of reality has itself become subject to lyric treatment, because it has become an intensely personal problem. It has often been so, perhaps, to the philosopher; but the generally felt historical extremity causing a universal calling into question of our basic cultural assumptions has become the stuff of human crises, has made the definition of reality as much the property of the poet and novelist as of the philosopher. That is, reality is no longer something we are given by virtue of accepted religious or political tenets, but something which we seem to be perpetually defining. Those who think about the moral and aesthetic fictions we live by are in quest of a new way or a refashioning of an old way. Witness the self-consciousness of the novelist who writes a novel about writing a novel, or the poet who writes a poem about writing a poem, or the philosopher writing philosophy about the methods of philosophy. Stevens engages in this revaluation of first principles, of traditional assumptions. He does so not as the programmatic theorist but as the inspired amateur, holding nothing more sacred than his idiosyncrasies. His first cause is temperament. Still, his self-consciousness delineates not only the movements of his own mind but of the changes in poetry as such.

In "Of Modern Poetry" he conveys his impression of the new source of value inherent to the poetry he writes. It begins with a distinction between the poetry which expressed attitudes which were already accepted and poetry which has had to promulgate its own subject matter.

> The poem of the mind in the act of finding
> What will suffice. It has not always had
> To find: the scene was set; it repeated what
> Was in the script.

But this way of writing, this dedication to an already organized view of reality, say in Spenser or Milton, gives way to a less exalted but more various aesthetic, which is centered upon actual rather than mythical actions.

> Then the theatre was changed
> To something else. Its past was a souvenir.
> It has to be living, to learn the speech of the
>   place.
> It has to face the men of the time and to meet

> The women of the time. It has to think about
>   war
> And it has to find what will suffice. It has
> To construct a new stage.

It is the self that becomes the stage, the drama, as the heroes become people who are not remote. They become yourself.

> It has to be on that stage
> And, like an insatiable actor, slowly and
> With meditation, speak words that in the ear,
> In the delicatest ear of the mind, repeat,
> Exactly, that which it wants to hear, at
>   the sound
> Of which, an invisible audience listens,
> Not to the play, but to itself, expressed
> In an emotion as of two people, as of two
> Emotions becoming one.

Those two inner people, readers of Stevens are not long in finding out, are imagination and reality, or reality as it appears to the perceiver. Modern poetry is a drama of the mind, the mind defining reality as it can, and in so doing creating it. In this sense the poet is the metaphysician, rather than the prophet or bard.

> The actor is
> A metaphysician in the dark, twanging
> An instrument . . . .

This is Stevens' image of the poet as thinker, the poem as meditation.

Yet this is a metaphysician whose conclusions have to do with gusto rather than reason. His conclusions may be a sensualist's parody of reason:

> Item: The green fish pensive in green reeds
> Is an absolute . . . .
>
> ("Montrachet-le-Jardin")

The concrete, particular experience is his absolute, as it is typically for the artist. Stevens is the opposite of peremptory in his reverse absolutism. Indeed, his "never-ending meditation" is qualified to the point of self-conscious caricature.

Of this
A few words, an and yet, and yet and yet —
("An Ordinary Evening in New Haven")

Or, to take another self-conscious caricature of one of his favorite and excessive modifications —

As if, as if, as if the disparate halves
Of things were waiting in a betrothal known
To none.
("Study of Images II")

Stevens' self-caricature is not confined to his style as a metaphysician, but is extended to his being a metaphysician at all. Not that he doubts the truth which his poetry expresses, but he is sometimes embarrassed by it. This situation is dramatized in the poem called "The Glass of Water," which begins, properly enough, with Stevens affecting a pedagogic style.

That the glass would melt in heat,
That the water would freeze in cold,
Shows that this object is merely a state,
One of many, between two poles. So,
In the metaphysical, there are these poles.

So much for the preliminaries. What the lesson is really about is the nature of a dialectic. We are supplied next with what is presumably a more illuminating example, an example which concerns poetry rather than physics.

Here in the centre stands the glass.
Light
Is the lion that comes down to drink.
There
And in that state, the glass is a pool.
Ruddy are his eyes and ruddy are his claws
When light comes down to wet his frothy jaws
And in the water winding weeds move round.

If this is a description of poetry and the dialectic of imagination and reality, it is also a caricature of poetry. The dialectic is too clearly drawn, the metaphors are too heavily underscored, too patently labeled, and the rhyme rhymes too much. The figure of the weeds disturbs the all too perfect picture. But this is only an anticipatory dissonance. The orderly dialectic explodes in an unseemly way.

> And there and in another state — the
>   refractions,
> The *metaphysica,* the plastic parts of poems
> Crash in the mind — But, fat Jocundus,
>   worrying
> About what stands here in the centre, not the
>   glass,
>
> But in the centre of our lives, this time,
>   this day,
> It is a state, this spring among the politicians
> Playing cards. In a village of the indigenes,
> One would have still to discover. Among the
>   dogs and dung,
> One would continue to contend with one's ideas.

The train of harmonious clarity is broken as the true metaphysics of imagination is revealed. More than a simple physical opposition, more than a calendar picture sense of poetry, poetry is seen here as a violent business. Fat Jocundus, the happy hedonist as sober metaphysician, transcends pat notions of his craft. For him, poetry has to do with reality as it manifests itself in the life that is lived in the scene composed around us. It is neither picturesque nor ennobling. It is, in fact, dull, homely, dirty. At his most ironic, then, the metaphysician tells us that the dialectic which yields truth for him is one which concerns violent ideas and imaginings and unpropitious facts. We are not far from the psychology of the dandy. The difference is that the poet no longer sees himself as alienated from society, but has his say in the thick of it. Refinement, for Stevens, is not enough. Much of his strength, like that of Williams and Marianne Moore, is linked to a pervasive absorption in the indigenous, come exhilaration or disgust.

The man embraces his masks, and there is no one guise which will do justice to the complexity of Stevens' vision. Although complexity is likely to be primarily an indication of the diverse claims which contemporary society makes upon the imaginative man and which the imaginative man makes upon society, it is in Stevens' case a sign of profundity as well. His masks, however playfully they are sometimes assumed, are not poses but the self-dramatization of urges deeply felt and insights intricately perceived. When he appears to be simple, it is with that simplicity which is, in Oscar Wilde's phrase, the last refuge of complexity. Like Whitman, Twain, Dostoevsky, Yeats, and Frost, Stevens presents himself through his writing as more than one self, fragmented as he is by the conflicting claims of conformity and revolt, acquiescence and expression, public claims and private impulses. What Richard Chase says of Whitman's masks holds true for Stevens' as well: "Like other modern writers Whitman found it temperamentally pleasurable as well as strategically necessary to interpose a half-ironic image of himself between the world and that profound part of his personality which hated figure and likeness"[19] — the spontaneous, the poetic, the iconoclastic impulses of the self.

The experienced reader of Stevens finds that his masks break down, in their variety, to related opposites: American Pan and weeping burgher, metaphysician and rationalist, rabbi and comedian, immaculate dandy and man on the dump, Fat Jocundus and the skinny sailor, the powerhouse and the man whose pharynx was bad. In each of these sets the first figure represents the man of imagination, who attempts to transcend or enhance the Hartford of his soul. The second figure represents the triumph of the quotidian, the confusion or the despair of the imaginative man, or at best, the poet as virtuoso lotus-eater. They reflect the conflict of a man who is both iconoclast and insurance executive, art collector and Hartford perambulator, realist and realtor, dandy and *haut* bourgeois.

A common criticism of Stevens' poetry is that there are no people in it. It is more accurate, if less grammatical, to say that Stevens is all the people in his poetry. His masks provide a sense of drama which other poets — Whitman, Frost, Eliot — achieve, in part, by a novelistic gift. This self-dramatization of his comic sense makes Stevens both wit and butt. Like the comic style of Laforgue and the early Eliot, Stevens' comic style is full of travesty and self-irony, full of integrations of the frivolous and serious. It is both a parody of a stately, grand style and a burlesque of the poet who cannot possess one. For Stevens is at once a leading modern exponent of an elevated style and one of its arch-enemies. The poet who wrote "Sunday Morning" and "Esthétique du Mal" also wrote "The Emperor of Ice-Cream" and "The Man on the Dump." There is a constant tension in his poetry

19. Richard Chase, *Walt Whitman Reconsidered* (London: Victor Gollancz Ltd., 1955), p. 42.

between the promulgation of a new seriousness and the deflation of a grandeur which he can see only as ridiculous. With dandiacal superiority, elegance, and detachment, he can wryly caricature the conventionally sacred, as in "Of Heaven Considered as a Tomb."

> What words have you, interpreters, of men
> Who in the tomb of heaven walk by night,
> The darkened ghosts of our old comedy?

In seeing history as a comedy Stevens is expressing what Laforgue and the early Eliot have felt before him, the sense of an absurd universe whose laws are surprising, nonsensical, farcical. Because of this sense of dilapidation, their poetry thrives on combining slang and astronomy, clownishness and erudition. Even in "Sunday Morning," where Stevens expresses a sense of harmony between man and the natural world, the wry line

> We live in an old chaos of the sun

inserts itself as a moderate version of the idea that life is an old comedy. Stevens is not really interested in the news from the tomb that the interpreters will bring, but in making a rowdy and elegant burlesque of the solemn.

> Make hue among the dark comedians,
> Halloo them in the topmost distances
> For answer from their icy Élysée.

In making a euphonious travesty of the exalted, Stevens indulges in his own kind of exaltation. To compensate for the lost grandeur there is his own hauteur.

There are times when the sartorial elegance of his verse makes eminently presentable the disarray of his feelings, as in "Le Monocle de Mon Oncle." If the poem is an inversion of elevated passion, it is also a tumultuously weary comment about the loss of this passion. The poem begins with a mock-heroic invocation which is half-parody and, it seems, half-nonsense.

> "Mother of heaven, regina of the clouds,
> O sceptre of the sun, crown of the moon,
> There is not nothing, no, no, never nothing,
> Like the clashed edges of two words that kill."
> And so I mocked her in magnificent measure.
> Or was it that I mocked myself alone?
> I wish that I might be a thinking stone.

These lines, in their progression from highest ethereal being to lowest corporeal being, are the self-conscious expression of a dandy who knows that effusions of passion are embarrassing and ludicrous, and that the lack of them threatens dehumanization. The last line quoted recalls the evolutionary regression fantasy of Prufrock, who wished that he were a pair of "ragged claws/ Scuttling across the floors of silent seas." The next stanza too recalls Eliot's lost soul.

> For it has come that thus I greet the spring.
> These choirs of welcome choir for me farewell.

Yet the remarkable thing about Stevens' poem to the longtime reader of Eliot is how different the two poems prove to be. Despite his initial self-castigation Stevens' persona is no Prufrock. The tone of Stevens' poem — with its subtle modulations of feeling and ridicule, wistfulness and composure, pain and confidence — and of the other Stevens poems which we have quoted, shows that he is essentially high-spirited and is engaged in a free laughter of the mind, though it is at times a defensive laughter. The difference between Prufrock and the middle-aged *oncle* is that the former feels old before his time. Stevens' protagonist has heard the voice of the sirens, and they still sing to him, despite his own sophisticated protestations and the reality of oncoming age. The dandiacal rhetoric of "Le Monocle" is the production of a fastidious energy which is far from being the prematurely dissipated energy which informs the mournful inter-rogatory accents of "Prufrock." The comic poetry of Eliot which comes closest to approaching Stevens' tone of satiric slapstick is his early, iconoclastic "The Hippopotamus" or "Cousin Nancy."[20] They share the intellectual high jinks and the irreverence which mark

20. An understanding of Stevens' debt to Eliot is complicated by the following assertion attributed to Stevens by William Van O'Connor: "At one time or another I have been under some great teachers but I have had only two Masters, and one of them is T. S. Eliot. My personal acquaintance with Eliot has been slight, being confined chiefly to correspondence; yet for about sixteen years I have been trying to learn everything from him that I can use." Actually, it was not Stevens who said this but Allen Tate. Stevens' remark about Eliot, appearing in the same number of the *Harvard Advocate*, is at once reverential yet far more detached and not without irreverence.

"I don't know what there is (any longer) to say about Eliot. His prodigious reputation is a great difficulty.

"While that sort of thing: more or less complete acceptance of it, helps to create the poetry of any poet, it also helps to destroy it.

"Occasionally I pick up Eliot's poems and read them, eliminating from my mind all thought of his standing. It is like having an opportunity to see, in an out of the

many of Stevens' comic poems. But Eliot does not usually laugh without terror — as in "Prufrock," "The Portrait of a Lady," "Mr. Appolinax," "Hysteria," "The Wasteland" — or disgust — as with Sweeny and Bleistein. As Wylie Sypher writes:

Stevens is endowed, as Eliot with his chill humor is not, with the Meredithian comic spirit, a mocking awareness of our absurdities and our pretense . . . . The comedy . . . is ringing with the silver laughter of the Meredithian faun; eruptive images, riotous language, springing delight over the victim, the intellectual tensions of *The Egoist*. The moments of high comedy in "Le Monocle" indicate how defensive are the ironies of *Prufrock*.[21]

Stevens' comedy is like Meredith's and Molière's in that it results in a laughter of the mind, a civilizing, if controversial, laughter. As Meredith in "An Essay on Comedy" says, "a cultivated society where ideas are current, and perceptions quick"[22] is required for this kind of laughter. There are no bellylaughs in Stevens, neither is there the laughter of despair. His wit and humor appeal to a cultivated, perhaps initiate, group who delight in the intellectual thrust and emotional subtlety it involves. But the similarity in comic spirit of Meredith and Stevens is not as close as Sypher's comment would indicate. To begin with, Meredith is more kindly disposed toward his victims; he seems to be personally involved with the faults of his characters. He writes, "Contempt is a sentiment which cannot be entertained by comic intelligence."[23] His laughable characters, for all their blind egotism or rigid thought, are treated with a thoughtful laughter which is chastening rather than derisive, in the last analysis. Meredith draws this distinction between comedy and satire: "The laughter of satire is a blow in the back or in the face. The laughter of comedy is impersonal and of unrivalled politeness."[24] The wit of Stevens, on the other hand, with all its subversive preferences, often takes a highly indecorous form. His laughter in poems like "A High-Toned

---

way place, a painting that has made a great stir: for example, it is like having a Giotto in what is called a breakfast nook.

"Reading Eliot out of the pew, so to speak, goes on keeping one young. He remains an upright ascetic in a world that has grown exceedingly floppy and is growing floppier." See William Van O'Connor, *The Shaping Spirit* (Chicago: Henry Regnery Company, 1950), pp. 45 f., and *The Harvard Advocate*, CXXV (Dec., 1938), 41-42.

21. Wylie Sypher, "Connoisseur in Chaos," *Partisan Review*, XII (Winter 1946), 94.
22. George Meredith, "An Essay on Comedy," pp. 3-57 of *Comedy*, ed. Wylie Sypher (New York: Doubleday Anchor Books, 1956), p. 3.
23. *Ibid.*, p. 3.
24. *Ibid.*, p. 33.

Old Christian Woman," "The Doctor of Geneva," and "The Emperor of Ice-Cream" is one of unrivaled impoliteness. Meredith's comedy is what is often called "English," a laughter of the heart and mind, a mingling of ridicule and pathos. Stevens, less kindly disposed towards his victims, unless that victim is an ironic projection of himself, laughs what Meredith calls "the polished Frenchman's mentally digestive laugh."[25] Stevens' humor, his comic sympathy, is restricted to the wry dramatization of his various masks and is extended in his later poetry to include his images of basic, if bedraggled, humanity. Here self-irony is the dominant tone, and as Meredith puts it, "Irony is the humor of satire."[26]

But even the masks of Stevens represent only rarefied though intense human beings, human beings recognized not by the fulness of a personal identity, but by the ideas they embody. That is, Stevens' method is the method of wit. He is hardly a humorist in his comedy at all. For the humorist, say Mark Twain or Sholem Aleichem, is committed above all to the world of particular people. His art is drenched in actuality — habits, mannerisms, customs, gestures. The humorist knows people so well that he can tell them things about themselves which they have long forgotten; or things which they have never had the insight and perspective wholly to understand. Stevens, on the other hand, does not present a drama of people as much as he does a drama of conflicting ideas. So traditional a source of the comic as the battle of the sexes is nowhere present. And although the fact that he is a lyric poet does not necessarily exclude what might be called novelistic dramatization — witness the characters of Eliot and Frost — in his poetry, Stevens is intimate only with the fascinating iconography of his own mind, and with its response to aspects of the general mind. Unlike Pope's wit, his is not the expression of common sense, welded in the indelible certitude of the heroic couplet. His wit is the opposite of common sense, and in this way, the opposite of what we think of as native American wit, the wit, as Irving Kristol describes it of "uncommon common sense . . . [which] is a standing challenge to, a perpetual refutation of, the book-learned, the cosmopolitan, the distinguished, the sophisticated."[27] Stevens is one of the avatars of American refinement and, as such, his writing, like James's

25. *Ibid.*, p. 40.
26. *Ibid.*, p. 44.
27. Irving Kristol, Review of *Mark Twain and Southwestern Humor*, by Kenneth S. Lynn, *Commentary*, XXIX (Feb., 1960), 169.

and Eliot's, is sophisticated, distinguished, cosmopolitan, and book-learned as can be. If his writing does not immediately strike one as American at all the reason is that, as Richard Chase once remarked, there is always something foreign about American elegance. Stevens' wit is far from being clear. It is hypercivilized, perverse, confusing and erudite. This does not mean that it will not endure. It may be apropos to recall Dr. Johnson's hasty judgment of another perverse, confusing, and erudite display of the comic spirit, *Tristram Shandy*: "Nothing odd will do long: *Tristram Shandy* did not last!"[28] Un-related as they are, much of the humor and wit of both Stevens and Sterne derives from a common motivation; the desire to exorcise obsolete and ridiculous ways of feeling and thinking for the sake of a new way which they truly felt. Their respective comic styles are, among other things, an exhibition of mock-erudition, pranks, sheer performance, irreverent jokes, obscurities, wilful outrage, and whirl-wind confusion. To add to this confusion, both Sterne and Stevens, along with self-conscious comedians like Byron and Laforgue, engage in self-parody as well as parody of everything else which they have reservations about, being as conscious of their own mannerisms, rigidities, and excesses as they are those of others.

But we do not get a full picture of Stevens' wit and humor if we lose sight of the fact that its calculated playfulness is compounded with a sense of extremity. Comedy is usually thought of as the chastising yet beneficent voice of society, taking the measure of those egoists or eccentrics who deviate from some norm of moral common sense. This is generally true for Molière and for Meredith. Bergson, with Molière as an example, thinks of comedy in terms of society breaking the absurd individual. Conversely, in "Laughter," he says, "You would hardly appreciate the comic if you felt yourself isolated from others. Laughter appears to stand in need of an echo."[29] Similarly, Meredith can say of the satiric Byron, "He had no strong comic sense, or he would not have taken an anti-social position, which is directly opposed to the comic."[30] But this is not so much a state-ment about the nature of comedy as it is a statement about the nature of comedy in Meredith. Meredith and Bergson do not take into account the many wits, often called romantic ironists, who see

28. James Boswell, *The Life of Samuel Johnson* (London: John Murray, 1889), VI, 79.
29. Henri Bergson, *Laughter*, pp. 61-190 of Sypher, *Comedy*, p. 64.
30. *Ibid.*, p. 44.

that the shams and absurdities of the world lie at the door of customs, conventions, and traditions which are disintegrating, and which society too readily accepts as eternal arbiters of taste and morality. Byron, Laforgue, and Stevens are such poets. Theirs is the wit of isolation. The striking thing about Stevens' "Ho-Hos" is that they are often their own lonely echo. Stevens' wit is like Laforgue's and Byron's in that it is subversive. It flouts the expected and conventional morality which Meredith's comedy endorses. And the expected taste — for in Stevens' arsenal is a rash and cunning variety of expression, derived, in part, from poets like Corbière, Laforgue, and Verlaine, which would be beyond the usually decorous Meredith. Stevens' poetry, and with it his comedy, came to birth as a result of the split in the teens and twenties between the man of taste and feeling and the general Babbittry. No less than writers like Gertrude Stein, Hemingway, and E. E. Cummings, though in an entirely different manner from all three, does he show his disillusion with merely public ideals and rhetorics. Their common genius was a literary intransigence. Wit deriving from this intransigence could not possibly have been the expression of society's common sense.

Although his world is not heavily populated with characters, Stevens' comedy embraces much of world consciousness. His wit, like Byron's and Laforgue's, like, for that matter, Hemingway's, fathoms for our delight and edification (or is it degradation?) not only the vagaries of literary tradition but the quirks of history, a history which, in our time, has made the word *absurd* fashionable. Perhaps our *Paradise Lost* will prove to be the grizzly *Waiting for Godot*, with its travesty of the second coming and the idea of a teleological universe. *Waiting for Godot* is significantly called a "tragicomedy" by Beckett; the distinction between the two has become obscured in that they no longer exclude each other. In Stevens, as in Laforgue and Eliot, there is the sense that the world is either dying or in the process of being reborn. Eliot turned to Anglo-Catholicism. Laforgue, alas, found the ridiculous above all in his own soul. Stevens' wit, although it is often directed at himself, is mainly directed at the fictions which have failed him. His brilliant comic sense has allowed him the boon of equilibrium, as he sifts out the old to come to the new. There is indeed feeling, if not always in the lines themselves, then between them.

*D*espite its imposing verbal surface, "The Comedian as the Letter C" is confessional, belonging to that class of literature popular in prose and in verse since *The Prelude* known as the spiritual autobiography. Wordsworth called it the "growth of a poet's mind." Without saying that "The Comedian" is strictly autobiographical even as a drama of consciousness, we may say that it is a comic projection of the incubation of a major comic talent. As we shall see, there are too many similarities between the poetic insights of Crispin and those of his creator to doubt the autobiographical element. The meaning of the poem, no less than its superfine style, is the expression of Stevens struggling for something unhackneyed to say, and for a startlingly original but honest way of saying it. There is honesty, to say nothing of wisdom, in the irony which juxtaposes the unadventurous everyday with an adventurous, gaudy, and grandly bizarre rhetoric. "The Comedian" is a masterful, if fanciful, expression of a wryly reflective sensibility, a mind struggling amidst a welter of poetic clichés to find its true style and contentment. Far from being an anomaly, "The Comedian" is characteristic Stevens, and could not have been written by anybody else.

The poem is about the struggle between man and the natural world, the conflict between individual will and intractable fate. But, in Stevens, if a poem is about man and his relation to his environment, it is also about his imaginative conception of this relation. It is a poem, then, about the relation of the imaginative man to the natural world and to his various imaginings of this natural world. It is a problematic relationship. First of all, because it is difficult to arrive at an imaginative rapport between self and world and secondly because the variety of myth employed is bewildering to the seeker of self-knowledge. Although the enterprise itself is heroic, Stevens treats it in mock-heroic fashion. For him, in this poem, the problems and pitfalls of this quest are much more tangible than its consummation. His hero is more a victim of fate than a masterful agent, and when he seems finally to be a masterful agent he is a conspicuous victim.

Crispin, the central character, is related to his namesake, the stock buffoon of French comedy. He is the comedian, the mock-learned projection of Stevens' poetic impulse. Yet the title remains cryptic. What is its sense? Why the letter C? Stevens answers this question in terms of the flamboyance of the language used in the poem, telling us that the title can be paraphrased as "The Comedian as the Sounds of the Letter C," adding to this remark a charming analysis.

You know the old story about St. Francis wearing bells around his ankles so that, as he went about his business, the crickets and so on would get out of his way and not be tramped on. Now, as Crispin moves thru the poem, the sounds of the Letter C accompany him, as the sounds of the crickets, etc. must have accompanied St. Francis. I don't mean to suggest that there is an incessant din, but you ought not to be able to read very far in the poem without recognizing what I mean. The sounds of the Letter C include all related or derivative sounds. For instance, X, TS, and Z. To illustrate in 'Bubbling felicity in Cantilene' the soft C with the change to hard C, once you notice it, ought to make that line a little different from what it was before. Sometimes the sound squeaks all over the place, as, for example, in the line 'Exchequering—' the word exchequering is about as full of the sounds of C as any word I can think of.[1]

Although the C is itself not minuscule, at one point Crispin is called "merest minuscule in the gales." He is small amidst the conflicting claims of poetry. "The Comedian" is a mock-heroic *Prelude*. Far from exalting a particular poetic mind, it shows a plain man — for despite his pretentiousness Crispin's desires are plain — lost in the conflicting claims of sensibility, who resolves his problem by giving them all up for a nice shady home and daughters with curls.

Commenting on "The Comedian," Stevens calls it "an anti-mythological poem."[2] By this he means what we have been calling the mock-heroic. As Stevens goes on to say, "the central figure is an everyday man who lives a life without the slightest adventure, except that he lives it in poetic atmosphere as we all do. This point makes it necessary for a translator to try to reproduce the everyday plainness of the central figure and the plush, so to speak, of the stage." There will be no claim made for man's kinship to the gods or even to the heroes of what might be considered storybook tradition. The central incongruity and source of comedy in the poem is precisely the juxtaposition of the everyday and our, alas, archaic, abortive impulse to rise highly above it. The comic deflation — vaguely glorious expectations coming to naught — is inevitable.

The poem begins with a statement typical of the old mythology.

> Nota: man is the intelligence of his soil,

a statement which is immediately qualified by Stevens' predisposition to caricature Platonic idealism.

> The sovereign ghost. As such, the Socrates
> Of snails, musician of pears, principium
> And lex.

The irony involved in being an intelligence over soil is typical of a poet accustomed to spoofing Plato and the worlds that exist beyond the soil. For Stevens, any account of man's exalted nature must include the conditions that are in large part going to determine that nature. Socrates perhaps; but Socrates of snails. Musician not of the spheres but of pears. The question arises

1. In a letter to Hi Simons dated Jan. 12, 1940.
2. Stevens, *Mattino Domenicale*, p. 169.

> ... is this same wig
> Of things, this nincompated pedagogue,
> Preceptor to the sea?

This answer is given in the wording of the question. How can a wig
of things, a man with a fraudulent top, a ludicrously pedantic fellow,
command the infinite, deep, wild sea of man's experience? Not well.
But he has made his attempts. His domestic intelligence, confronted
with the vastness of experience, has gone obscurantist:

> An eye most apt in gelatines and jupes,
> Berries of villages, a barber's eye
> An eye of land, of simple salad-beds,
> Of honest quilts, the eye of Crispin, hung
> On porpoises, instead of apricots,
> And on silentious porpoises, whose snouts
> Dibbled in waves that were mustachios,
> Inscrutable hair in an inscrutable world.

Thrust out on the sea of experience his barber's eye meditates on
silentious[3] porpoises as he forsakes homey experience for absorption
in the mystery. He is sophomoric in his new speculations and
absolutely Byzantine in his newly found elegance.

> One eats one paté, even of salt, quotha.

His experience is to be much less elegant than his first imaginings
will allow. Still, in his first flush of imaginative enthusiasm, he is
not sorry for having forsaken his "eye of land."

> It was not so much the lost terrestrial,
> The snug hibernal from the sea and salt ...
> What counted was mythology of self
> Blotched out beyond unblotching ....

Whatever his regrets for having left the land of honest quilts, he has
done it for a more important fate. This fate is nothing less than
finding a new self, the old self being forgotten beyond any possibility
of recall. Crispin is not raised in stature by virtue of this decision. He
has had the courage to strip himself of a stale motley identity, but
he feels his new nakedness.

3. A coinage; since it is Crispin who is observing them, these notoriously carefree
sea-dwellers are wrapped in an aura of pretentious silence.

>   . . . Crispin,
> The lutanist of fleas, the knave, the thane,
> The ribboned stick, the bellowing breeches, cloak
> Of China, cap of Spain, imperative haw
> Of hum, inquisitorial botanist,
> And general lexicographer of mute
> And maidenly greenhorns, now beheld himself,
> A skinny sailor peering in the sea-glass.

Unheroic to begin with, he is especially aware of his present puniness. Far from possessing a new identity, he is lost, overwhelmed by the flood of new experience.

> Crispin was washed away by magnitude.

Musician of pears and lutanist of fleas, even this clinquant cunning deserts him in his new experience. The stanza ends with a dissonance reflecting his lack of mastery.

> The whole of life that still remained in him
> Dwindled to one sound strumming in his ear,
> Ubiquitous concussion, slap and sigh,
> Polyphony beyond his baton's thrust.

Crispin, a child of the *Sturm und Drang* of the twenties, abandons the land of honest quilts and salad beds; as J. V. Cunningham observes, Stevens elsewhere describes this scene as "the comfortable American state of life in the '80's and '90's and the first ten years of the present century," a time characterized by business, public chastity, and official Christianity — or what we call Victorianism.[4] Along with it he has abandoned the traditional poetry of the time. The problem of finding a new self becomes one with finding a new poetic style.

The sea is experience and the totality of poetic style as well. The second stanza makes this clear. The unruliness of the sea is seen to be a special kind of disorder. It is the chaos of an old poetic style. It is the verboseness of old mythologies which gave rise to Crispin's conjectures about inscrutable hair in an inscrutable world. The first stage in Crispin's evolution after the domestic is the verbosity of old myth.

4. J. V. Cunningham, "The Poetry of Wallace Stevens," *Poetry*, LXXV (Dec., 1949), 155.

> Could Crispin stem verboseness in the sea
> The old age of a watery realist,
> Triton, dissolved in shifting diaphanes
> Of blue and green? A wordy, watery age
> That whispered to the sun's compassion, made
> A convocation, nightly, of the sea-stars,
> And on the clopping foot-ways of the moon
> Lay grovelling.

At first, Crispin cannot stem this verboseness, as phrases like "silentious porpoises" and "inscrutable hair" testify. Triton's age, here generically the age of the grand myths, was wordy in that it lived by the no longer valid beliefs in the sun's compassion and convocations to the sea-stars. These are the imaginings that Stevens deflates. Crispin takes Triton for a deity, but it is Triton at a vast remove from his original force and significance. It is

> Triton incomplicate with that
> Which made him Triton, nothing left of him,
> Except in faint, memorial gesturings,
> That were like arms and shoulders in the waves,
> Here, something in the rise and fall of wind
> That seemed hallucinating horn, and here,
> A sunken voice, both of remembering,
> And of forgetfulness, in alternate strain.

What exists of Triton for us today is Triton minus that which made him such a meaningful Triton once. Only the pale memorial gesturings of the old myths are left. We are left with an expressionistic picture of Triton's dissolution.

The third stanza begins on a note of resolution. The old Crispin, the one who espoused the old myths, is dissolved just as Triton himself is. The stock character valet in the tempest of old rhetoric is forgotten. It is a new Crispin who makes his jaunt to the Yucatan, although still a Crispin of an unheroic mold.

> Crispin, merest minuscule in the gales,
> Dejected his manner to the turbulence.
> The salt hung on his spirit like a frost,
> The dead brine melted in him like a dew

Of winter, until nothing of himself
Remained, except some starker, barer self
In a starker, barer world, in which the sun
Was not the sun because it never shone
With bland complaisance on pale parasols,
Beetled, in chapels, on the chaste bouquets.

This is a description of Crispin's third incarnation. In this starker
world, the sun's indifference replaces the sun's compassion. In place
of the chaste bouquets is the stripping away of all sentimentality.
Crispin becomes a mind which sees starkly, clearly through illusion.
Crispin now confronts what he thinks is reality — a reality which is
unadorned, austere.

Here was the veritable ding an sich, at last,
Crispin confronting it, a vocable thing,
But with a speech belched out of hoary darks
Noway resembling his, a visible thing,
And excepting negligible Triton, free
From the unavoidable shadow of himself
That lay elsewhere around him.

The plain world of material fact speaks to him but in a way unlike
his own more windy manner. Crispin is free, however, from fancy
Platonic sovereign ghosts, "the unavoidable shadow of / himself," although there does remain some vestigial "negligible Triton." We
must make no mistake about his basically new identity, however.

                              Severance
Was clear. The last distortion of romance
Forsook the insatiable egotist. The sea
Severs not only lands but also selves.
Here was no help before reality.
Crispin beheld and Crispin was made new.
The imagination, here, could not evade,
In poems of plums, the strict austerity
Of one vast, subjugating, final tone.
The drenching of stale lives no more fell down.

The comforting distortions of romance, the myths about the "sun's
compassion" and the "foot-ways of the moon," forsake Crispin. The

austerity of his newly found experience is the austerity of disillusion. He settles now for reality, material reality, poems of plums. The staleness of his past life is behind him. He calls it

> The ruses that were shattered by the large.

By "the large," he means immanence of the physical world, the vast presence which he now confronts. This confrontation is typical of the movement of Stevens' mind. This first section of the poem is subtitled *The World Without Imagination*. It presents us with an image of just that. It is the old imagination which is stripped away. It is not so much stripped away by Crispin as it is stripped away from him. Experience imposes itself on him and he is left in the end with a reality of objects, "something given to make whole." It is still a world without imagination.

The second section of the poem begins as a continuation of the last stanza of the first. Crispin is now an initiate to the pangs and buffets of imaginative growth. His vision is beginning to take shape. Seeing through the ruses of imagination is itself an act of imagination. Behind every no is the promise of yes. There is still more for Crispin to reject. We find him at the apex of his journey from Bordeaux; we find him in the Yucatan, the southernmost point of his journey, the point of the most abundant natural felicity. In Mexico too Crispin finds imaginative distortion of natural reality, despite the lushness of this reality, despite this green South.

> In Yucatan, the Maya sonneteers
> Of the Caribbean amphitheatre,
> In spite of hawk and falcon, green toucan
> And jay, still to the night-bird made their plea,
> As if raspberry tanagers in palms,
> High up in orange air, were barbarous.

Despite the rather exotic birds of everyday, the Mayan sonneteers are still enthralled by the mysterious nightingale or its equivalent, symbol of an ineffable essence which is a bane to the grasping of reality. Reality, as Stevens depicts it, leaves us breathless in its natural splendor. The "raspberry tanagers in palms,/ High up in orange air" is one of those exhilarating tableaus of natural reality which Stevens is a master at portraying. But the Mayan sonneteers, still under the influence of the nightbird, mistake the truly marvelous for the barbarous. Avoiding common reality, they court the ineffable. This seeking the rare and strange is commonplace, whereas the seizing of common day itself is rare by comparison. When Stevens writes

> But Crispin was too destitute to find
> In any commonplace the sought-for aid

he is saying that the lyrics to the tantalizing bird of night are the commonplaces. They are stale props of the imagination, and of no interest to the denuded Crispin. Crispin has left the old self which responded to such props behind. The sea has purified him, washed him clean.

> He was a man made vivid by the sea,
> A man come out of luminous traversing,
> Much trumpeted, made desperately clear,
> Fresh from discoveries of tidal skies,
> To whom oracular rockings gave no rest.
> Into a savage color he went on.
> How greatly had he grown in his demesne,
> This auditor of insects!

Crispin's quest has led him on to intense progress indeed. From his early conventional verse, the product of a conventional imagination —

> He that saw
> The stride of vanishing autumn in a park
> By way of decorous melancholy; he
> That wrote his couplet yearly to the spring,
> As dissertation of profound delight.[5]

5. Judging from his very early verse and his comment about it, there is every reason to believe that Stevens is indulging in self-irony here. Selections from his undergraduate verse are to be found in *The Harvard Advocate Anthology* (New York: Twayne Publishers, 1950). It is unfair, but I will quote one sonnet in its entirety and the last six lines of another.

> Lo, even as I passed beside the booth
> Of roses, and beheld them brightly twine
> To damask heights, taking them as a sign
> Of my own self still unconcerned with truth;
> Even as I held up in hands uncouth
> And drained with joy the golden-bodied wine,
> Deeming it half-unworthy, half divine,
> From out the sweet-rimmed goblet of my youth;

— to his new awareness is a violent passage. The new Crispin

> Stopping, on voyage, in a land of snakes,
> Found his vicissitudes had much enlarged
> His apprehension, made him intricate
> In moody rucks, and difficult and strange
> In all desires, his destitution's mark . . . .

Having broken with the traditional he becomes, in his stark aloneness, an outcast of the imagination. Crispin has developed that inner
violence without which there is no imaginative survival from the
outer violence of a society which impinges upon imagination. His
imaginative violence manifests itself in an apparently unpoetic way,
or so it may seem to the traditionalist. He forsakes the nightingale,
the ineffable, the sentimental stupor, to grasp the natural world of
common colors and events.

> His violence was for aggrandizement
> And not for stupor, such as music makes
> For sleepers halfway waking. He perceived
> That coolness for his heat came suddenly,
> And only, in the fables that he scrawled
> With his own quill, in its indigenous dew,
> Of an aesthetic tough, diverse, untamed,
> Incredible to prudes, the mint of dirt,
> Green barbarism turning paradigm.

The wheel has come full circle. Once a prude himself, he now comes

---

Even in that pure hour I heard the tone
Of grievous music stir in memory,
Telling me of the time already flown
From my first youth. It sounded like the rise
Of distant echo from dead melody,
Soft as a song heard far in Paradise.
                                         (p. 65)
Like this he pondered on the world's first day,
Sweet Eden's flowers heavy with the dew;
And so he led bold Jason on his way
Sparkling forever in the galley's foam
And still he shone most perfect in the blue
All bright and lovely on the hosts of Rome.
                                         (p. 66)

The latter is a poem about the morning star. This poetry is redeemed by Stevens'
comment: "Some of one's early things give one the creeps" (p. 6).

to challenge conventional, prudish taste with a tough aesthetic —
tough-minded and tough to swallow — based on the beauty of natural
objects. Stripped of the sentimental, he wallows in actuality. Rather
than indulge in a polemic against the dominant prudery, Stevens
makes the mock-heroic heroic. Because Stevens knows that Crispin's
thought and feeling are unacceptable, perhaps incomprehensible, except to the initiate of the modern, he articulates Crispin's awareness
with the wry self-irony and exhilarating difficulty which only the modernist would find inviting. Crispin is unpoetic because the poetic is
false. Dirt, not cleanliness, is next to godliness for him. The newly acquired logic of his life stems from green barbarism, rash, unrefined
indulgence in the actual. But at the very height of this indulgence
in the sweet wildness of green barbarism Crispin envisions even
a further stripping away to naked reality. Uneasy with the riches
in the mint of dirt, he senses

> . . . beautiful barenesses as yet unseen,
> Making the most of the savagery of palms,
> Of moonlight on the thick cadaverous bloom
> That yuccas breed, and of the panther's tread.

The "veritable ding an sich" becomes not so much lush natural reality
as the quest for a more basic kind of reality. Crispin must ultimately
reject "the fabulous and its intrinsic verse." In this South of perpetual
green Crispin does not find an aesthetic tough enough to satisfy his
craving for an anti-poetic poetry, for a poetry free of the shackles of
the traditionally poetic. The Yucatan is one of those Southern para-
dises, one of those insular Tahitis (Melville's phrase from *Moby
Dick*), that Stevens loves to wallow in, for the sensations it conveys
and for the answer it provides to those who do not like to think of
life on earth in physical terms. But for Stevens, this abundant South
is not enough. He is not one for an insular Tahiti. Like the hero of
Melville's *Typee* he is a Western man who must ultimately forge a
Western self, a tough consciousness which does not evade the am-
biguities of existence. Both Stevens and Melville are tough-minded
and attempt to pierce clearly down to the nature of reality (though
the nature of reality in each case is, of course, quite different). Stevens,
then, foregoes the attraction of the South for a Northern vision of life.
This is the dialectic geography of "The Comedian," and it is a move-

ment of mind more typical of *Harmonium* than some distinguished critics have been led to believe. Louis Martz, for example, taking "Nomad Exquisite" as the typical poem in *Harmonium*, interprets the volume as a kind of modern "Lotus-Eaters," with the poet reversing Tennyson's staunch superiority to such attractions. Martz finds himself in the position of having to say that "Farewell to Florida," the opening poem of "Ideas of Order," represents a rejection of *Harmonium*, represents Stevens assuming a new identity.[6] But it is not nearly as much a rejection of *Harmonium* as a projection of some of its most characteristic ideas. Stevens knows and loves too well the attractions of the physical world not to be wary of its excesses. His stand on this matter is of course as far from Puritan as one can be. But it is also far from mere hedonism. When Stevens says farewell to the South and hails the North in "Farewell to Florida," he is dramatizing a situation which is not new for him. Although he says farewell to the South in his poem, he is to return to it with pleasure again and again, though with less frequency and abandon than in *Harmonium*. "Farewell to Florida" posits this simple antithesis between North and South, an antithesis which sheds clear light on the development of "The Comedian." Florida is a mistress he must forget. His Northern reincarnation is not something out of a fairy tale. As in "The Snow Man," the stripping away of illusion is accompanied by a barrenness of landscape. Assuming the Northern role is a formidable thing, a violent reaching of the mind toward naked reality.

> Her mind had bound me round. The palms were hot
> As if I lived in ashen ground, as if
> The leaves in which the wind kept up its sound
> From my North of cold whistled in a sepulchral South,
> Her South of pine and coral and coraline sea,
> Her home, not mine . . .
> . . . .
> I hated the weathery yawl from which the pools
> Disclosed the sea floor and the wilderness
> Of waving weeds. I hated the vivid blooms
> Curled over the shadowless hut, the rust and bones,

6. Louis Martz, "The World as Meditation," *English Institute Essays*, 1957 (New York: Columbia University Press, 1958), pp. 143-158.

> The trees like bones and the leaves half sand, half sun.
> To stand here on the deck in the dark and say
> Farewell and to know that that land is forever gone
> And that she will not follow in any word
> Or look, nor ever again in thought, except
> That I loved her once . . . Farewell. Go on,
>   high ship.

Meanwhile back in the Yucatan — we find Crispin making a conversion of a similar kind. His movement Northward is far less violent (although it is Northward it will be only as far north as Carolina) just as his view of the South is not so bitter. Nevertheless Crispin rejects the lush South, "the fabulous and its intrinsic verse," a world "too juicily opulent." Crispin seeks a more tenable, a more basic reality.

> The affectionate emigrant found
> A new reality in parrot-squawks.
> Yet let that trifle pass.

Crispin is making a transition between the too opulent South and the North. The loss of his Southern identity is underscored by the physical action in his adventure. For as in the first section, Crispin is washed away. First it was the sea of experience itself; here it is a storm which performs the symbolic baptism. Crispin is purified once more, but there remains something still to be purged. Although he has made the most of the savagery of palms, his sense of "an elemental fate" which will draw him to "beautiful barenesses as yet unseen" predominates. This fate first takes the form of an eloquent thunderstorm. Crispin, inspecting façades, runs for shelter.

> He knelt in the cathedral with the rest,
> This connoisseur of elemental fate,
> Aware of exquisite thought. The storm was one
> Of many proclamations of the kind,
> Proclaiming something harsher than he learned
> From hearing signboards whimper in cold nights.

Crispin is scared into an epiphany. The thunder convinces him that his aesthetic is not yet tough enough. Nor will the domestic knowledge gleaned from signboards be of much help in his new quest. Here is a force having to do with the mystery, "the quintessential fact."

> He felt the Andean breath. His mind was free
> And more than free, elate, intent, profound
> And studious of a self possessing him,
> That was not in him in the crusty town
> From which he sailed.

So ends the second phase of the growth of a poet's mind. We now follow him northward, in *Approaching Carolina*,[7] section three. He moves toward America, Northern land.

> America was always north to him,
> A northern west or western north, but north,
> And thereby polar, polar-purple, chilled
>
> . . . . .
>
> And cold in a boreal mistiness of the moon.
> The spring came there in clinking pannicles
> Of half-dissolving frost, the summer came,
> If ever, whisked and wet, not ripening,
> Before the winter's vacancy returned.

Here then is the new climate conducive to inner winter weather. An unsentimental vision of life and a correspondingly unsentimental poetry is what Crispin is after. Toward this poetry Crispin necessarily makes many sacrifices.

> How many poems he denied himself
> In his observant progress, lesser things
> Than the relentless contact he desired;
> How many sea-masks he ignored; what sounds
> He shut out from his tempering ear; what thoughts,
> Like jades affecting the sequestered bride;
> And what descants, he sent to banishment!

Like Stevens, Crispin engages in the stripping away of old forms and beliefs. Yet the difference between Stevens and his persona, Crispin, becomes gradually clear. For where Stevens continues to evolve as a poet, Crispin comes to give up poetry altogether. Crispin, as we shall

7. In the first section of the poem we are told that he plans to stop at Havana; but this is a journey of consciousness and the slip makes no difference.

see, finds the quotidian to be adequate to his quest. He is not a perpetual adventurer in reality. At the very height of his new-found awareness, Crispin, unlike Stevens, feels hesitant about committing himself to the imagination of the North, the imagination of disillusion.

> Perhaps the Arctic moonlight really gave
> The liaison, the blissful liaison,
> Between himself and his environment,
> Which was, and if, chief motive, first delight,
> For him, and not for him alone. It seemed
> Illusive, faint, more mist than moon, perverse,
> Wrong as a divagation to Peking,
> To him that postulated as his theme
> The vulgar, as his theme and hymn and flight,
> A passionately niggling nightingale.
> Moonlight was an evasion, or, if not,
> A minor meeting, facile, delicate.

The imagination of the North seems to give him the oneness between self and environment that he desires. But then like the lush moonlight world of the Yucatan, it seems to offer not enough. He still lives in a world of moonlight, of the myth of imagination. This seems to be an evasion to a man who desires relentless contact with the most common elements of existence. We find Crispin unresolved, trying to find some enduring relationship between imagination (moon) and reality (sun).

> Thus he conceived his voyaging to be
> An up and down between two elements,
> A fluctuating between sun[8] and moon. . . .

To the degree that Crispin indulges his fancy in an element which he no longer fully feels, he is displaying weakness. Despite these fluctuations Crispin has his goal in mind.

> But let these backward lapses, if they would,
> Grind their seductions on him, Crispin knew
> It was a flourishing tropic he required

8. Reality is symbolized, conventionally enough, by the sun; elsewhere ("Gubbinal," "The Brave Man") the sun is a symbol, again a fairly conventional one, of vital energy.

> For his refreshment, an abundant zone,
> Prickly and obdurate, dense, harmonious
> Yet with a harmony not rarefied . . . .

Crispin wants something more than the bareness of the North, now
that he sees it. Also an atmosphere of refinement is inadequate. He
wants a plainness, but not like any he has yet seen or imagined.

> And thus he tossed
> Between a Carolina of old time,
> A little juvenile, an ancient whim,
> And the visible, circumspect presentment drawn
> From what he saw across his vessel's prow.

The Carolina of old time is, I think, the seductive, pretty fictions
which Crispin has all but completely rejected. The "circumspect pre-
sentment" is the new Carolina, the Carolina he is now approaching.
It is quite different from an evasive moonlight meeting now. Here,
despite Crispin's doubts, is the desired vulgar at last, the inversion of
what is ordinarily considered poetic, "the passionately niggling nightingale."

> He came. The poetic hero without palms
> Or jugglery, without regalia.
> And as he came he saw that it was spring,
> A time abhorrent to the nihilist
> Or searcher for the fecund minimum.
> The moonlight fiction disappeared. The spring,
> Although contending featly in its veils,
> Irised in dew and early fragrancies,
> Was gemmy marionette to him that sought
> A sinewy nakedness.

Here is the unheroic hero in all his lack of splendor; without palms,
without regalia, mistrustful of fair weather and the season of romance. All his imaginative fictions, from the Yucatan to the Arctic,
are discarded. At last he is face to face with arrant reality.

> A river bore
> The vessel inward. Tilting up his nose,
> He inhaled the rancid rosin, burly smells

Of dampened lumber, emanations blown
From warehouse doors, the gustiness of ropes,
Decays of sacks, and all the arrant stinks
That helped him round his rude aesthetic out.
He savored rankness like a sensualist.
He marked the marshy ground around the dock,
The crawling railroad spur, the rotten fence,
Curriculum for the marvelous sophomore.
It purified. It made him see how much
Of what he saw he never saw at all.

Stevens descends to the depths of eloquence, as it were, to find words
adequate to the unheroic quality of his hero's quest. Once more
Crispin is purified, this time by a vision of reality so basic, so irreducible, that there can be no more common denominator. Crispin sees
at last that man, far from being a Platonic ghost, or romantic hero,
derives his being from the relentless contact with the rudeness of our
contemporary world. Our sense of beauty must come from this rudeness, this caricature of our unheroic world. Crispin is made to encounter reality head on. Just as Stevens must make the man with
poetic impulses appear ridiculous, he must make the poet's reality
seem rank. Rankness is the tribute his aesthetic pays to beauty. He
feels a sense of liberation.

He gripped more closely the essential prose
As being, in a world so falsified,
The one integrity for him, the one
Discovery still possible to make,
To which all poems were incident, unless
That prose should wear a poem's guise at last.

Falsified as the intelligence is by notions of man's elevated nature in
a noble world of ideas, it becomes a mark of true distinction to be
enamoured of the base. Heroism being false, one must embrace the
unheroic; poetry being merely poetic, one must preserve the integrity
of prose in verse. Crispin is honest, therefore perverse. Stevens is in
sympathy with his mock-hero insofar as he writes a verse which stems
from the situation of the modernist poet; he must, in J. V. Cunningham's phrase, "Exasperate the reader or succumb to him."[9]

9. Cunningham, *Poetry*, p. 151.

Crispin settles for the poetry of humble, even smelly objects. His choice is outrageous to one who has a sense of poetry as part of an ennobling tradition having to do with heroes, gods, and flowers. Stevens is degrading, and in being so indulges a modern predisposition. It is a predisposition which is well described by William Barrett; "When the modern sculptor disdains the pomp of marble and uses industrial materials, steel wire, or bolts, or even rejected materials like old board, rope, or nails, he is perhaps showing himself to be impoverished next to the heroic grandeur of a Michelangelo, but he is also bringing us back to the inexhaustible brute world that surrounds us."[10] Stevens shares in this discarding of traditional consciousness, even though he preserves the traditional forms to a considerable extent in his familiar, meditative, conventional, iambic pentameter verse. There is no doubt, however, that the burden of Stevens' message, as well as that of his most original verse techniques, is distinctively modern. "The Comedian" is a choice example of this modernity.

We left Crispin, the marvelous sophomore, inhaling the gustiness of ropes, gripping life's essential prose. The transition from life as poetry to life as prose has been made. Life in its intractable thingishness, in its common brute mundaneness, is the stage for our hero. The glorious assertion with which the poem began — "Man is the intelligence of his soil" — is so muted by the successive stages of Crispin's development that it becomes its comic inversion. The fourth section of the poem begins:

> Nota: his soil is man's intelligence,
> That's better. That's worth crossing seas to
> find out.

Having temporarily come to terms with his environment or his fate — for in Crispin's case his environment is his fate — Crispin seeks a scene adequate to his experience and meditation. The marvelous sophomore wishes to have his ideas realized by means of the concretion of social reality.

> Crispin in one laconic phrase laid bare
> His cloudy drift and planned a colony.

10. William Barrett, *Irrational Man* (New York: Doubleday, 1958), p. 40.

To be sure it is a social reality which is to be realized in Crispin's mind and as an instance of his new knowledge rather than in any intrinsically social sense. In any case, the vicissitudes of imagination are left behind, now that a prosy truth has been arrived at.

> Exit the mental moonlight, exit lex,
> Rex and principium, exit the whole
> Shebang. Exeunt omnes. Here was prose
> More exquisite than any tumbling verse:
> A still new continent in which to dwell.

The promise of the last line in the preceding section becomes more and more the province of prose, prosy experience. In his anti-mythological world, prose is more eloquent than "any tumbling verse." He clearly prefers his new awareness to the hackneyed poeticism with which he started his journey. Indeed his purpose is to show the obsolescence of the opposing view.

> What was the purpose of his pilgrimage,
> Whatever shape it took in Crispin's mind,
> If not, when all is said, to drive away
> The shadow of his fellows from the skies,
> And, from their stale intelligence released,
> To make a new intelligence prevail?

The opposing view is sufficiently caricatured and generalized to cover a multitude of sins. But what counts for the reader is not the special individuality of the old but the unique quality of the new. The "stale intelligence" has to do with the proposition that man is the intelligence of his soil. Crispin's modest fatalism rejects that view and sees the soil as man's intelligence, sees man as a creature of the formidable world of natural things and objects. And of the even more formidable world of the anti-mythological.

> Hence the reverberations in the words
> Of his first central hymns, the celebrants
> Of rankest trivia, tests of the strength
> Of his aesthetic, his philosophy,
> The more invidious, the more desired;
> The florist asking aid from cabbages,
> The rich man going bare, the paladin

> Afraid, the blind man as astronomer,
> The appointed power unwielded from disdain.

Each of Crispin's examples points to holes in the armor of the way things should be according to storybook tradition. The world of customary expectations is stood on its head. His perverseness and disdain are the measure of his intelligence. He couples this disdain with the "appointed power" — the verbal gift that every poet must have. The line is a good definition of the comic.

The other side of Stevens' disdain is a program for the future based on the "new intelligence." Striving for some reconciliation between man and his overwhelming surroundings, Crispin envisions his colony. It is a colony which will have the characteristic quality of the place from which it springs. It is an earthly venture and will, however many attempts are made to disguise the fact, have an earthly tone. Naturally, there will be as much variety in the colony among people as there will be among places, the people differing just as the places differ.

> The man in Georgia waking among pines
> Should be pine-spokesman. The responsive man,
> Planting his pristine cores in Florida,
> Should prick thereof, not on the psaltery,
> But on the banjo's categorical gut,
> Tuck, tuck, while the flamingoes flapped his bays.
> Sepulchral señors, bibbling pale mescal,
> Oblivious to the Aztec almanacs,
> Should make the intricate Sierra scan.

Etcetera. All of which proves that his soil is man's intelligence. We do not hear the music of the psaltery — medieval sound — but of the "banjo's categorical gut." The newer sound is clear and necessary in a secular era. The mummery of Aztec almanacs is forgotten as the intricacies of the actual Sierras become the subject matter of verse. Ritual becomes the expression not of faith but of reason.

> The melon should have apposite ritual,
> Performed in verd apparel, and the peach,
> When its black branches came to bud, belle day,
> Should have an incantation. And again,
> When piled on salvers its aroma steeped

> The summer, it should have a sacrament
> And celebration.

Here, in a light mood, Stevens' reverence for the natural is seen in the secular use of religious terms — like "ritual," "incantation," "sacrament," "celebration," and "novitiates." Nobody else could have written "The melon should have apposite ritual." Much of his poetry is the finding of this suitable ritual.

In the *Adagia*, Stevens says, "Reality is the object seen in its greatest common sense." The growth of Crispin's mind is very much the growth of a private common sense. The more he experiences in the way of skeptical revelation, the more possible a life becomes for him. Common sense becomes a cardinal virtue when the world talks nonsense. Crispin elevates common sense to the position of grace. A priest of the commonplace, he senses the need for followers.

> Shrewd novitiates
> Should be the clerks of our experience.

Despite his vicissitudes, Crispin's development is consistent. He is always aware of his building his argument in opposition to a generic poetic tradition, a tradition which he sees as false to the facts of existence. His notions about a colony are yet another aspect of this awareness. The impulse which prompts him to his claims for a naturalistic reality is the obverse of his early false conceptions.

> These bland excursions into time to come,
> Related in romance to backward flights,
> However prodigal, however proud,
> Contained in their afflatus the reproach
> That first drove Crispin to his wandering.

Crispin is in a position to summarize what his mediocre past now means.

> He could not be content with counterfeit,
> With masquerade of thought, with hapless words
> That must belie the racking masquerade,
> With fictive flourishes that preordained
> His passion's permit, hang of coat, degree
> Of buttons, measure of his salt. Such trash
> Might help the blind, not him, serenely sly.
> It irked beyond his patience.

What the old myths ultimately pointed to was an inscrutable order of predestined things and events. For Stevens, its ultimate meaning is its ultimate failure. It is ridiculous to think that there is a providence in the fall of a sparrow. The juxtaposition of the idea of predestination with the little things that make up life lends itself readily to caricature. Worst of all, the falsely comforting "hapless words" of the old myths make very small man's chances to attain some mastery of self and environment in this difficult life, in "the racking masquerade." Falsifying the macrocosm, it murders the microcosm. Crispin rejects the trash. Impatient with moralizing, he has restlessly set out upon the sea of experience.

> Hence it was
> Preferring text to gloss, he humbly served
> Grotesque apprenticeship to chance event,
> A clown, perhaps, but an aspiring clown.

Crispin is a clown not only because he falls on his face once every so often, but because he subjects himself to special ridicule by the violence of his quest for reality. The energy of this quest makes him a gay clown rather than a sad one. He is after all a rarity — a tough-minded clown. The opposite of the sentimental clown, he rejects the wish-dream for a tougher but better reality.

> There is a monotonous babbling in our dreams
> That makes them our dependent heirs, the heirs
> Of dreamers buried in our sleep, and not
> The oncoming fantasies of better birth.
> The apprentice knew these dreamers. If he dreamed
> Their dreams, he did it in a gingerly way.
> All dreams are vexing. Let them be expunged.
> But let the rabbit run, the cock declaim.

Rejecting the mere dream, he gives himself with abandon over to freedom, instinct, actuality. Crispin's tough-mindedness takes the form of arduous honest writing. He is not one of those poetic fakers who serve up a jumble of inflated rhetoric based on the old dreams and relics.

> Trinket pasticcio, flaunting skyey sheets,
> With Crispin as the tiptoe cozener?
> No, no: veracious page on page, exact.

The fourth section concludes then with an image of Crispin making his book with the same painstaking effort of a dandy making his wardrobe. The verse of the poem is indeed that of a dandy. Hypercivilized, ironic, and unique, it assiduously attempts to suffuse into modern life a vividness, a gaudiness, a gaiety which it sadly lacks. Stevens' striking vocabulary, a kind of Brummell American, a mixture of the latinate and the colloquial, the precious and the wild, is a joyous yet nervous answer to the national sameness. A connoisseur in discontent and expert in the knowledge of boredom, the dandy contrives the most ingenious and affected ways to transform this reality into something splendid. Stevens' verse, in this poem and in many of the other early poems, is an example.

In "The Comedian" Stevens' comic projection of himself, Crispin, achieves a sense of honest perplexity but it is a perplexity which he is incapable of resolving. Crispin is a clown and clowns are not allowed the victories of profound reflection and exalted emotion. As we might expect, the comedian becomes the victim of his own profundity.

His development takes a new turn in the fifth section, called *A Nice Shady Home*. The action which follows is not as bland as the subtitle would indicate. Indeed, the irony of the title's simplicity becomes increasingly apparent the more we read. Nevertheless, there is a certain relaxation of Crispin's will. It is a fatalistic relaxation, which distinguishes Crispin from Stevens. Crispin assumes a new role. There are two reasons for this. First, having dispelled in his own mind the power of the mythological, he (unlike Stevens) no longer has the confident energy of discontent to carry him to further iconoclastic adventures concerning the nature of reality.

> Crispin as hermit, pure and capable,
> Dwelt in the land. Perhaps if discontent
> Had kept him still the prickling realist,
> Choosing his element from droll confect
> Of was and is and shall or ought to be,
> Beyond Bordeaux, beyond Havana, far
> Beyond carked Yucatan, he might have come
> To colonize his polar planterdom
> And jig his chits upon a cloudy knee.
> But his emprize to that idea soon sped.

A prosy realist, he settles for the extreme of prosy realism, a nice

shady home. It is an extreme to which the best energies of so many
in our society are directed that one seldom realizes the nature of one's
extremity. Not so Crispin. No longer "the prickling realist" struggling
with "was and is and shall or ought to be," he has given up the idea of
actually forming a colony. A typically comic intelligence, he has become too much the skeptic to plan even so modest a Utopia. He is a
realist who settles for the way things are, as far as the social patterns
of his society are concerned. In this Crispin is conspicuously like
Stevens. How many poets would find Parnassus in Hartford? Who but
Stevens was a master of verse technique and surety bonds?[11] Like
Stevens, Crispin becomes subject to the attrition of the everyday.

> Crispin dwelt in the land and dwelling there
> Slid from his continent by slow recess
> To things within his actual eye, alert
> To the difficulty of rebellious thought
> When the sky is blue. The blue infected will.

The second reason for Crispin's newly assumed identity is propin-
quity. Once he has made his decision to dwell inland, this decision
reinforces itself by the new circumstances of his existence. The blue
sky here has the early connotation, not of imagination, but of the
given in life — its peace and limitation.[12] Crispin's retreat inland marks
his retreat from the labors of modern poetry. He feels a sense of anti-
climax.

> . . . day by day, now this thing and now that
> Confined him, while it cosseted, condoned,
> Little by little, as if the suzerain soil
> Abashed him by carouse to humble yet
> Attach. It seemed haphazard denouement.

If I unscramble the syntax here rightly, his new mundane existence, the
existence of the soil, ingratiates itself with his ego. In a playful way
it humbles his former ambitious self, while the newer identity is made
to attach itself to its new surroundings. This is no great dramatic conclusion. It is somewhat inconclusive, the way the comic denouement
frequently is. Nevertheless, there is a consolation; Crispin has grown.
Even if he is a realist *manqué*, he is a realist.

11. Stevens, says Hartford Accident & Indemnity President Wilson Jainsen, "was
renowned as a specialist in surety bond work." *Time*, Aug. 15, 1955, p. 12.
12. See "Le Monocle de Mon Oncle" VI, "Sunday Morning" III.

> He first, as realist, admitted that
> Whoever hunts a matinal continent
> May after all, stop short before a plum
> And be content and still be realist.
> The words of things entangle and confuse.
> The plum survives its poems. It may hang
> In the sunshine placidly, colored by ground
> Obliquities of those who pass beneath,
> Harlequined and mazily dewed and mauved
> In bloom. Yet it survives in its own form,
> Beyond these changes, good, fat, guzzly fruit.
> So Crispin hasped on the surviving form,
> For him, of shall or ought to be in is.

He has come to the conclusion that reality is the world we live in, and the objects that compose it. Simple in itself, almost pitifully simple, it marks a radical departure from his earlier concern with "inscrutable hair in an inscrutable world." Indeed it marks a sharp departure even from the poems of plums which Crispin had earlier intended to write. For now, Crispin is more intent upon the plums than the poems about them. In fact he develops a mistrust for words altogether. To the extent that Crispin is Stevens, he is a poet in spite of himself writing a poem about the inadequacy of poetry, decrying the inadequacy of words in an outpouring of verbal opulence. In Stevens himself there is the desire to take the actual object as the *ding an sich,* and to come to terms with the quotidian. But unlike Crispin, Stevens does not become a victim of the quotidian. Despite a lapse of a few problematic years after the publication of *Harmonium* in which Stevens wrote no poetry, he becomes a connoisseur of the quotidian, coming to terms with it only after he has made it imaginatively his own. For Stevens, social reality is often too dull, and the object unaided by the imaginative perception of it is not enough. Crispin has given up on an imaginative energy which Stevens was always to trust and to cherish. Crispin stops writing poetry, Stevens does not. To be sure, Stevens was for a long time to be enchanted by "good, fat, guzzly fruit." The "is" is of the first importance to him but, unlike Crispin, he never forgets the "shall" and "ought," the attempt to see the "is" in a meaningful way.

Crispin does not have the energy required for poetry. He no longer has the will to come to an imaginative conclusion concerning the world and his place in it. Haphazard denouement will have to do. This is not an heroic theme, and cannot be sung in sonorous verse.

> Was he to bray this in profoundest brass
> Arointing his dreams with fugal requiems?
> Was he to company vastest things defunct
> With a blubber of tom-toms harrowing the sky?
> Scrawl a tragedian's testament? Prolong
>
> His active force in an inactive dirge,
> Which, let the tall musicians call and call,
> Should merely call him dead? Pronounce amen
> Through choirs infolded to the outmost clouds?
> Because he built a cabin who once planned
> Loquacious columns by the ructive sea?
> Because he turned to salad-beds again?
> Jovial Crispin, in calamitous crape?

Here Crispin ruminates upon the irony of his quest. He seems to be right back where he started from. His plans for a true poetry are gone, but the salad-beds endure forever. Crispin becomes something of a fatalist, but a modest one at that. There is no somber poetic requiem here, no pompous song to the sky, no tragedy. The old songs cannot be reactivated. Crispin is too modest to serve as a hero, too ironic to serve as a martyr.

> Should he lay by the personal and make
> Of his own fate an instance of all fate?
> What is one man among so many men?
> What are so many men in such a world?
> Can one man think one thing and think it long?
> Can one man be one thing and be it long?
> The very man despising honest quilts
> Lies quilted to his poll in his despite.
> For realist, what is is what should be.

As is often the case with the comic hero, in contradistinction to the tragic hero whose fate should be intelligible as the moral order of the universe in which he lives, his adventures have led him nowhere. The return to the normal is cause for the note of celebration with which traditional comedies conclude. In the romantic ironist Stevens, however, it is a stale normality which is the subject of ridicule to begin with. Crispin is to be applauded not so much for his return as for his self-imposed exile. He is never more the clown than at the moment of his reunion with the conventional. Crispin proves to be what Bergson calls the "dancing jack,"[14] the comic marionette whose freedom is only apparent. What is real is his embarrassment, his loss of face, his surrender to the quotidian. But Crispin's fate is not simply that of a pathetic clown. He was an "aspiring clown" and is not to be laughed at. He is too conscious of himself and of his predicament to be considered a fool; indeed, he convinces us of the laughableness of society in its inert and ready-made conventions. The comedian at his best, and Crispin is this, is, in Wylie Sypher's phrase, "the self behaving as prodigal and bohemian."[15] If we must smile at Crispin's fate, we must also admire his energy. His peregrinations may be devoid of definitive actions but his mind is dominated by a significant attitude. He has experienced the quest of the imaginative man for reality; and if he has not seized upon a truth, he has, deservingly, stumbled in the direction of one. He is far from being the histrionic obscurantist he once was. Indeed, his insights have the perplexing virtue of being tentative.

Coralled by the comforts of the everyday, Crispin's tired but still active imagination settles for a realism of a most literal and unspectacular kind. His quest for the *ding an sich* finds its abrupt conclusion in bourgeois life. Though Crispin is pinned to honest quilts, he can see his predicament with a measure of imaginative insight. The mark of this insight is his disillusion; another mark is his new role. Although he resists it, Crispin is presented with a happy ending. The first heroic aspect of Crispin's bourgeois rejuvenation is his becoming "magister of a single room," one he shares with his "prismy blonde." His new routine has its virtues indeed. He finds himself

> . . . in a round
> Less prickly and much more condign than that
> He once thought necessary. Like Candide,
> Yeoman and grub, but with a fig in sight,
> And cream for the fig and silver for the cream
> A blonde to tip the silver . . . .

14. Bergson, *Laughter*, pp. 111 ff.
15. Sypher, "The Meaning of Comedy," pp. 193-255 of *Comedy*, p. 241.

But his old speculative self is reasserted wistfully.

> Yet the quotidian saps philosophers
> And men like Crispin like them in intent,
> If not in will, to track the knaves of thought.

Crispin had both the intent and the will to arrive at a truth which would make a peace between himself and the world. Like Stevens' famous man whose pharynx was bad, Crispin no longer can sing of his adventures. He has stopped writing poetry. He too feels the malady of the quotidian. The clutter of daily experience, charming and erotic at its best, saps the philosopher. But Crispin is an amateur philosopher and does not go down with his system. Essentially the comedian, Crispin cannot let things go without a laugh. The nincompated pedagogue wryly contemplates his new treasure.

> For all it takes it gives a humped return
> Exchequering from piebald fiscs unkeyed.

If I understand these lines rightly — and there is a meaning to these words in addition to their surface elegance — Crispin meditates here on the diabolical slyness of the conditions of quotidian existence. For all that it requires of us, its return is grotesquely less than we expect. So it is that the quotidian taxes motley (in the sense of common) personal treasuries with a disregard that amounts to lawlessness.

The sixth section makes us realize that the anti-climax of the fifth section (*A Nice Shady Home*) was a climax after all. It is called *And Daughters With Curls*. Crispin has no less than four.

> The return to social nature, once begun,
> Anabasis or slump, ascent or chute,
> Involved him in midwifery so dense
> His cabin counted as phylactery . . . .

Although he is not sure whether his return to social reality is an advance or a regression — how problematic is the fate of the thinking man in our society! — he is, once more, caught up by an elemental fate which seems to decide things for him. Once again Crispin is washed away by magnitude; here experience manifests itself in very concrete forms — four daughters. His cabin counted as phylactery; that is, it was a reminder of his obligation to keep the law (in this

case the law of natural reality). Thus Crispin's uneasy peace with the
natural world becomes more and more of a reality. He partakes of the
natural life cycle, a cycle which receives one of its best expressions
in the familiar lines from Stevens' "Peter Quince at the Clavier":

> The body dies; the body's beauty lives.
> So evenings die, in their green going,
> A wave, interminably flowing.

The particular body is part of the cycle of natural life, which includes
the reality of physical beauty; just as one evening leads to the beauty
of another, changing yet remaining the same; just as one wave, ex-
hausting its brilliance, yields to the oncoming sameness of the sea.
This is why Stevens describes Crispin's chits as

> Infants yet eminently old . . .
> Green crammers of the green fruits of the world . . . .

The infants are beginning the cycle of life, starting at once their
indulgence in the actual (which is signified as usual by the color
green). The charm of the chits draws a smile from domesticated
Crispin.

> Effective colonizer sharply stopped
> In the dooryard by his own capacious bloom.

Faced as he is by a welter of growth, Crispin becomes an "indulgent
fatalist." Confronted by the elemental realities, he submits to their
charms. His daughters stand as four naturalistic furies, a turbulent
vendetta imposed upon one who would flout the social idea from
which they sprung, the mystique of simple salad-beds and honest
quilts. What, then, is the moral of the story?

> Crispin concocted doctrine from the rout.
> The world, a turnip once so readily plucked,
> Sacked up and carried overseas, daubed out
> Of its ancient purple, pruned to the fertile main,
> And sown again by the stiffest realist,
> Came reproduced in purple, family font,
> The same insoluble lump. The fatalist
> Stepped in and dropped the chuckling down his craw,
> Without grace or grumble.

Reality, hard, unyielding, the turnip, the insoluble lump, crams itself down Crispin's throat. He swallows it managing to be civil. As in "The Man Whose Pharynx Was Bad," a symbolic oppressive purple permeates the scene. Although Crispin had once stripped the world of its tenacious dullness, arriving at an exotic basic reality, the grim realist is once again confronted with the immovable haze of the quotidian. At best, Crispin's intentions have been open and noble; these verses therefore appear as

> Seraphic proclamations of the pure
> Delivered with a deluging onwardness.

Or so Crispin would like them to appear. But if it strikes the reader that Crispin is the same knave we had confronted at the outset of his tergivizations, perhaps he must admit to a fate not pristine.

> . . . if the music sticks, if the anecdote
> Is false, if Crispin is a profitless
> Philosopher, beginning with green brag,
> Concluding fadedly, if as a man
> Prone to distemper he abates in taste,
> Fickle and fumbling, variable, obscure,
> Glozing his life with after-shining flicks,
> Illuminating, from a fancy gorged
> By apparition, plain and common things,
> Sequestering the fluster from the year
> Making gulped potions from obstreperous drops,
> And so distorting, proving what he proves
> Is nothing, what can all this matter since
> The relation comes, benignly, to its end?

Perhaps Crispin has been not much more than the thinking man's braggart warrior. Surely he is one of those heroes whose quest is of greater interest than their goal; he is at best a modern comic Faust, not heroic but almost anonymous, a minuscule, a letter C. Like Kafka's heroes who go by the letter K, he is an instance of the modern predicament in which the power of the self to determine its plain fate seems to be minuscule indeed. The world about us — in its substantiality of opposing institutions and conflicting myths — looms so incredibly large as the determining factor in our existence that the self seems to get lost in trying to understand it. Crispin's adventures do not end conclusively. But comedy is valued not so much for its conclusions as for the questions it presents. His fate is not so important as the conditions which determine it. Besides, his adventures do come benignly to their end. Stevens ends the tale, saying

So may the relation of each man be clipped.

underscoring the fact that the modern self must settle for no grand conclusions.

Chapter 3: The Sacred Irreverence of Wallace Stevens

hen we say that poetry is modern we mean two things. First, that it is a new poetry, one which stands in opposition to poetry which has come before it and receives much of its creative impetus from its flouting the attitudes implicit in the old poetry. This is what we may call the absolute sense of the word modern. Donne, Wordsworth, Coleridge, and Whitman were modern poets. The author of "The Comedian as the Letter C" is modern in this sense. He blames some of the failures of the present on the fictions of the past, fictions which seem to him caricatures of the meaning they once possessed. But he is also modern in the second sense of the word, the historical sense. Stevens' poetry is characteristic of recent times, the past fifty years. It is concerned with the breakdown of belief, the moral wasteland, the pressures of materialistic realties on the life of the imagination. Twentieth-century poetry is largely a difficult poetry appealing to a relatively small audience of presumably discriminating readers. It has had to confront the attitudes of a society which is largely antipathetic to poetry and therefore shares with absolute modern poetry a resistance of taste and belief which is the given circumstance of its inception. The absolute modern of the twentieth century is perhaps the modern poet par excellence, since no other poet has encountered the attitudes of the past with such a total response, a past which has never been more ubiquitous as a cultural presence, whether as a challenge, as in Eliot, or a comedy, as in Stevens.

Of course, the historical modern poet, the poet of the twentieth century, need not be an absolute modern. Edwin Arlington Robinson, Yvor Winters, and J. V. Cunningham are twentieth-century poets who are conservative in their poetry. To be sure, Stevens too has been influenced by the versification of the past. As Cunningham has pointed out, "Sunday Morning" is parasitic on what it rejects in that it assaults the traditional in traditional language.[1] But no one is more conspicuously modern than Stevens. When he writes in his *Adagia*, "The poet is a god, or, the young poet is a god. The old poet is a tramp,"[2] he is expressing his absolute modernity; he is casting his lot with the new, with *brio*, with the assault on the past. Although much more gaudy and gay, Stevens is as serious as Wordsworth in this assault. Too much has been made of Stevens as the relaxed traveler with a remarkable ear for poetry in his off-hours. Too much has been made of his hedonism. While he is, to be sure, a devotee of the gods of pleasure, he is also a deeply reflective poet. No one is more aware of the role of poetry in a secular epoch. In commenting on his striking stylistic perversity, criticism has generally disregarded the serious subversiveness of his ideas. Although his outlook is sanguine, from the point of view of a more conventional morality and taste it is in many ways heretical. The generalized heterodoxy of "The Comedian" becomes more explicit in other poems. Stevens' heterodoxy is one of the most striking features of his modernity.

"The labor of modern culture," says William Barrett in his recent survey of existential philosophy, *Irrational Man*, "wherever it has been authentic, has been a labor of denudation. A return to the sources

1. Cunningham, *Poetry*, p. 162. Also, see Cunningham on the use of the word "modern."
2. Stevens' *Adagia* is found in *Opus Posthumous*, pp. 157-180.

... toward a new truthfulness, the casting away of ready-made pre-
suppositions and empty forms."[3] However different they may be in
other respects, Stevens and the existentialists share this attitude. Like
the existentialists, Stevens wants to bring man back to the irreducible
facts of his existence. Like them, he refuses to adorn the old sou-
venirs. His disparagement of moralism, his deflationary style, Sartre
would admire. The poem "Lions in Sweden" is a case in point.

> No more phrases, Swenson: I was once
> A hunter of those sovereigns of the soul
> And savings banks ....

A constant source of Stevens' satiric wit is the juxtaposition of outdated moral idealism and the mundane contemporary scene, symbolized here by the lions and their presence at the front of a bank. A
mock-heroic catalogue follows:

> ... Fides, the sculptor's prize,
> All eyes and size, and galled Justitia,
> Trained to poise the tables of the law,
> Patientia, forever soothing wounds,
> And mighty Fortitudo, frantic bass.
> But these shall not adorn my souvenirs,
> These lions, these majestic images.

Stevens believes that the supreme fictions which man creates, for
example the classical and Christian fictions which have made Loyalty,
Justice, Patience, and Fortitude supreme values, are the fictions by
which the soul is formed. These values are the object of satire here.
It is not the idea of a supreme fiction that Stevens rejects, but the
old fictions which are no longer supreme. This sort of grievance can
be most effectively stated by a man who is himself a moralist, whose
desire for a supreme fiction is great. He is most aware of the lack of
one.

> If the fault is with the soul, the sovereigns
> Of the soul must likewise be at fault, and first.
> If the fault is with the souvenirs, yet these
> Are the soul itself.

3. Barrett, *Irrational Man*, p. 35.

The sovereign images or supreme fictions are the soul of a civilization itself. This has never changed. But the particular images have changed.

> . . . And the whole of the soul, Swenson,
> As every man in Sweden will concede,
> Still hankers after lions, or, to shift,
> Still hankers after sovereign images.
> If the fault is with the lions, send them back
> To Monsieur Dufy's Hamburg[4] whence they came.
> The vegetation still abounds with forms.

The last naturalistic twist is typical Stevens. For Stevens, the sovereign images must be created through the interaction of man's imagination and man's natural environment. Unlike T. S. Eliot, Stevens has no notion of reconstructing morality through the church. Stevens has referred to himself as a "dried-up Presbyterian";[5] whatever we may think of the intensity of Eliot's Anglo-Catholicism, there is certainly a genuine effort at conversion. For Eliot, if the fault is with the soul, it is not because the fault is with the sovereign images. He sees the past as more sinned against than sinning. Where Stevens would try to create a new fiction Eliot would like to see an old one dominant once more.

The tone of the old sovereign images bothers Stevens — the purity, the aloofness, the pomp — as typified by swans. They arouse his genteel invective, in the poem "Invective against Swans."

> The soul, O ganders, flies beyond the parks
> And far beyond the discords of the wind.

4. Cf. Guillaume Apollinaire, *Le Bestiaire*, illustré par Raoul Dufy (Paris: La Sirene, 1919), n.p. Dufy has caricatured pompous public statues on other occasions, but the caricature here is on the part of Apollinaire, whose quatrain on "Le Lion" is thematically similar to "Lions in Sweden."

> O lion, malheureuse image
> Des rois chus lamentablement,
> Tu ne nais maintenant qu'en cage
> A Hambourg, chez les Allemands.

How degrading it is for these proud fellows to pace up and down in their square cages at the Hamburg zoo; as degrading perhaps as saying cheese in front of a savings bank. But for Apollinaire this is no less ridiculous than the lamentable regal image they once embodied.

5. Bernard Heringman, "Wallace Stevens: The Reality of Poetry" (unpublished Ph.D. dissertation, Dept. of English, Columbia University), p. 35 n. Stevens says this in a letter dated July 21, 1953.

That is, the soul transcends the place of the swans and other discordant surroundings. "Ganders" here means male goose but also a dull or stupid person. Stevens continues:

> A bronze rain from the sun descending marks
> The death of summer, which that time endures
>
> Like one who scrawls a listless testament
> Of golden quirks and Paphian caricatures,
>
> Bequeathing your white feathers to the moon
> And giving your bland motions to the air.

"Bronze" in Stevens connotes something which has the reality of things as they are in their natural cycle. Like the words "sun" and "summer" it signifies actuality, experienced life. Stevens is saying that summer endures its own death in the perpetual natural cycle just as a scribe endures the death of the testament or holy book he is writing in the cycle of religious systems. Stevens is typically irreverent in describing the holy books as "golden quirks and Paphian caricatures," as eccentric flashes of insight and comedies of unlawful sexual indulgence, in which the immaculate swan absurdly figures in holy ethereal imaginings. But this is not all:

> Behold, already on the long parades
> The crows anoint the statues with their dirt.
>
> And the soul, O ganders, being lonely, flies
> Beyond your chilly chariots, to the skies.

The statues, like the swans symbolic of old sovereign images, are being anointed by outrageous reality. Beyond the figurative meaning, the tableau of dirty statues and jilted swans is a funny one. The soul is left, not with heaven and its remote, grandiose sanctity, its chilly chariots of swans, but with its own loneliness and the skies.

"Academic Discourse at Havana" also makes capital of the swan as swan-song, the obsolescence of religious pomp. Here too is a poem about the new inheritance; the natural is valued as the real, the sundry of our lives takes the place of the miraculous and the ineffable.

> Canaries in the morning, orchestras
> In the afternoon, balloons at night. That is
> A difference, at least, from nightingales,

> Jehovah and the great sea-worm. The air
> Is not so elemental nor the earth
> So near.
> > But the sustenance of the wilderness
> Does not sustain us in the metropoles.

The earth is not so near because it cannot be addressed in personal
terms. One no longer speaks of the handiwork of God, or the chariot
of Apollo. Stevens makes no concessions about the difficulty of being
in a secular time. The miracles of the wilderness, say, manna, have
no relevance to the merely human predicaments of metropolitan
existence. This modern condition is not always a cause of celebration
in Stevens, as the void left by the deflation of the old myths is not
necessarily an easy one to contemplate. The next stanza begins with
a line which could have been written by the melancholy Laforgue:

> Life is an old casino in a park.
> The bills of the swans are flat upon the ground.
>
> . . . .
>
> The swans . . . Before the bills of the swans
> > fell flat
> Upon the ground, and before the chronicle
> Of affected homage foxed so many books,
> They warded the blank waters of the lakes
> And island canopies which were entailed
> To that casino . . .
>
> . . . .
>
> The indolent progressions of the swans
> Made earth come right; a peanut parody
> For peanut people.

The allusion to "the chronicle/ Of affected homage which foxed so
many books" is very close in sense to the "listless testament/ Of
golden quirks and Paphian caricatures" of "Invective against Swans."
The era of the chronicle is the era of the swans. It was the tune
played in the casino. It meant harmony for those who, in Stevens'
view, evaded the adventure of selfhood. He irreverently calls them
"peanut people." The moral universals upon which their myth de-
pended Stevens sees as a fantasy begotten in the scholar's insomni-
ous night, having less relevance to the way things are in the various

natural world than to an infatuation with universal truth. The natural
world, as is frequently the case in Stevens, is signified by a Southern
place, in this case Cuba.

> . . . The world is not
> The bauble of the sleepless nor a word
> That should import a universal pith
> To Cuba. Jot these milky matters down.
> They nourish Jupiters.

The dandy Stevens treats this foray into the history of ideas with
proper detachment and levity, referring to his ideas as "milky matters,"
and adding with the parenthetical nonchalance of historical disillusion that this is the stuff that gods are made of. Stevens concludes this
academic discourse, this reasoned lecture, with the pedagogue's hope
that the poet will find the ideals once embodied in the deflated
swans.

> How pale and how possessed a night it is,
> How full of exhalations of the sea . . .
> All this is older than the oldest hymn,
> Has no more meaning than tomorrow's bread
> But let the poet on his balcony
> Speak and the sleepers in their sleep shall
>   move,
> Waken, and watch the moonlight on their
>   floors.
>
>   .   .   .   .
> And the old casino likewise may define
> An infinite incantation of our selves
> In the grand decadence of the perished swans.

The only universal meaning that the new poet's message will have
is the meaning of simple, worldly things, imaginatively perceived.
The song will not be hymns but songs of ourselves.

Unlike Baudelaire in his memorable "Le Cygne," Stevens has no
nostalgia for the paradise lost symbolized by the majestic swan.
Baudelaire despairs of ever finding paradise again, but Stevens thinks
that paradise is not something to be found again but something to
be lost once and for all, or, at best, a paradise on earth to be made
anew. Stevens never despairs in the religious sense of the word; he

never becomes alienated from God and from self, thereby giving up hope of hope. For Stevens there is no personal God to be alienated from; rather there is a sense of man's aloneness in the coldness of space. This sobering realization, this symbolic winter of the mind, is earliest expressed in "The Snow Man."

> One must have a mind of winter
> To regard the frost and the boughs
> Of the pine-trees crusted with snow:
>
> And have been cold a long time
> To behold the junipers shagged with ice,
> The spruces rough in the distant glitter
>
> Of the January sun; and not to think
> Of any misery in the sound of the wind. . . .

Stevens wants man to have a mind of winter, a mind which must be clear, even cold, to penetrate beyond the sham of illusion. The illusion which Stevens particularly has in mind here is the pathetic fallacy, that poetic device which assumes a personal relationship between man and the world. In "Lycidas," for example, the shepherd is one with Nature; they share the same response, both weeping at the death of Lycidas. Stevens does not share in this kind of exaltation. The choirs of flowers are reduced to

> . . . the sound of a few leaves,
>
> Which is the sound of the land
> Full of the same wind
> That is blowing in the same bare place
>
> For the listener . . . .

Indeed, the listener himself shares in this stripping down to bare reality.

> . . . the listener, who listens in the snow,
> And, nothing himself, beholds
> Nothing that is not there and the nothing
> that is.

Words like "bare," "nothing," and, in other poems, "naked," "barren," "empty" — found conspicuously in "Evening Without Angels" and other poems — are witness to the relentless process of stripping away and reconstruction in which Stevens engages. The old illusion is continually being swept away; but the new reality is not an easy one. The last lines of "The Snow Man" are a statement of existential nothingness, which, as in Sartre, is human consciousness, the mode of being of human existence. The snow man is nothing himself, beholding the nothing that is not there — that is, making none of the old assumptions. And, gazing upon the snow and winter trees, he beholds the nothing that is — that is, he confronts reality even in its barrenness.

The firmness of Stevens' desire to get back to the roots of human experience, to make a new start for the mind, is the reason why his wit can be as effective as it is. He can deflate an old myth with gusto because there is a new one to support him and with *brio* because he is a clown of language. He laughs with bravado, even in, especially in, the most sacred places. The much sung story of garden and angel, too vulnerable for having been too long the subject of rhymers, is subjected to expansive foolery by a wit who has been disturbed by its reverberating euphony. This is Eden revisited on a merry-go-round.

> The garden flew round with the angel
> The angel flew round with the clouds,
> And the clouds flew round and the clouds
>   flew round
> And the clouds flew round with the clouds.

The harmonious order of the universe, for long a subject of much elevated rhetoric, is travestied in a poem of flip, jazzy gaiety. The final bit of circulating is designed to put the circle-of-perfection myth out of circulation. When under the impact of the new science, John Donne lamented the breaking of the circle of perfection, that medieval *gestalt* of universal harmony, it was very moving. But Stevens finds it less than moving that some men are still bound in belief by such symbols. In the next stanza he writes:

> Is there any secret in skulls,
> The cattle skulls in the woods?
> Do the drummers in black hoods
> Rumble anything out of their drums?

Where the circle was once seen as including all, Stevens sees it as a circle which is delimiting. He sees things as they are obscured by a hullabaloo of spiritual secrecies. Carrying his assault from perfection of the universe to perfection of the racial or national type, he continues to see the circle as something which typically excludes rather than includes.

> Mrs. Anderson's Swedish baby
> Might well have been German or Spanish
> Yet that things go round and again go round
> Has a rather classical sound.

The word "classical," as used by the people who wish to perpetuate the myth of racial purity, is loaded with vagueness, with inarticulateness, with nonsense; it has this in common with what the drummers rumble.

The atmosphere of mysterious jumble and thrum also pervades that funny funereal poem, "Cortège for Rosenbloom." The reader is alerted by the very title with its juxtaposition of just plain Rosenbloom with the word *cortège*, which has perhaps a connotation of exclusiveness. But the event is not exclusive or noble. The processional is buglike, the iterated rhyme a parody of that harmony which comes with final rest.

> Now, the wry Rosenbloom is dead
> And his finical carriers tread,
> On a hundred legs, the tread
> Of the dead.
> Rosenbloom is dead.
> . . . . . .
> The tread of the carriers does not halt
> On the hill, but turns
> Up the sky.
> They are bearing his body into the sky.

If one may insert a stage direction, the last line should be read with some astonishment. The image of the bugs entering the vault of heaven bearing "the wry Rosenbloom" on high is Stevens at his irreverent best. The procession continues:

> It is the infants of misanthropes
> And the infants of nothingness
> That tread . . .

> To a chirr of gongs
> And a chitter of cries
> And the heavy thrum
> Of the endless tread
> That they tread;
>
> To a jangle of doom
> And a jumble of words
> Of the intense poem
> Of the strictest prose
> Of Rosenbloom.
>
> And they bury him there,
> Body and soul,
> In a place in the sky.
> The lamentable tread!
> Rosenbloom is dead.

The bearers are called "infants of misanthropes" and "infants of nothingness" in performing this act. They are engaged in a cause which is hateful to man as Stevens understands him, a finite creature in a natural world which has no before and after. They are perpetuating the old, the myth of "a place in the sky." This is why the tread is "lamentable." They are violating simple reality, the embodiment of the ordinary, "the intense poem of the strictest prose."

"The Death of a Soldier" also treats the theme of death with wit but in a more serious manner. Despite the somber sincerity of the piece, Stevens' irreverence cannot be kept down.

> Life contracts and death is expected,
> As in a season of autumn.
> The soldier falls.
>
> He does not become a three-days
>   personage,
> Imposing his separation,
> Calling for pomp.

The allusion to "a three-days personage" is an allusion to the myth of Christ. The soldier's death is seen as nothing special, but part of life as we know it. It is therefore capable of moving us. Death for Stevens does not involve the question of eternal life but is "absolute and without memorial." Stevens attempts to clinch his argument with a beautiful description of what death is like in terms of our natural environment. We see death as something we know, as part of the rhythm of natural life. Eternal and ephemeral as the clouds, human life goes on.

As we have said in relation to "Lions in Sweden," Stevens does want sovereign images, but sovereign images forged out of an imaginative apprehension of the natural, the vegetation which still abounds in forms. That this will not be easy work Stevens knows. He sees too much, has too much a sense of proportion, a sense of humor, to state such an enormous proposition without some self-irony. In "Mud Master," it is difficult to perceive the forms of vegetation, the icons of the naturalistic mythology.

> The muddy rivers of spring
> Are snarling
> Under muddy skies.
> The mind is muddy.
>
> As yet, for the mind, new banks
> Of bulging green
> Are not;
> Sky-sides of gold
> Are not.
> The mind snarls.

The possibilities are great, but not always clear. But Stevens is a man of faith, and proclaims this faith to the man who counts, basic humanity in its lowest common denominator.

> Blackest of pickanines,
> There is a master of mud.
> The shaft of light
> Falling, far off, from sky to land,
> That is he —
> The peach-bud maker,
> The mud master,
> The master of the mind.

Considering the shaft of light, the peach bud and mind itself, Stevens perceives the source of his sovereign image, the earth itself. In this

poem mud is to Stevens what the rainbow is to Wordsworth. Stevens'
heart can leap up for more quotidian substances. Indeed, Stevens can
see even a soldier-hero in the same uncharismatic light.

> Unless we believe in the hero, what is there
> To believe? Incisive what, the fellow
> Of what good. Devise. Make him of mud,
> For every day.

> ("Examination of the Hero in a Time of War" VI)

Stevens is making an aesthetic of earth, real earth.

Of course Stevens is not always so *terre à terre.* "Ploughing on Sunday," the day people used to rest on, makes a point similar to the one
made in "Mud Master" in an outburst of hilarity, and in a cadenced
verse that is as buoyant as the experience itself.

> Remus, blow your horn!
> I'm ploughing on Sunday,
> Ploughing North America.
> Blow your horn!

> Tum-ti-tum,
> Ti-tum-tum-tum!
> The turkey-cock's tail
> Spreads to the sun.

> The white cock's tail
> Streams to the moon.
> Water in the fields.
> The wind pours down.

As in Laforgue's "Dimanches," Stevens uses Sunday as a counter-
point to the meaning it once had, a profoundly meditative counter-
point in "Sunday Morning" and an exuberantly jocular one in
"Ploughing on Sunday." The sheer exhilaration of the experience of
"Ploughing on Sunday" calls for a special vocabulary. One cannot
have such victory without a musical flourish. It is as if Stevens, in his
assault on tradition, were adding insult to injury by inserting drum
noises instead of poetical language. It is irreverence being jubilant at
its success. This is simply another aspect of Stevens' modernity.

The assault on deity becomes alarmingly specific in "The Blue

Buildings in the Summer Air." Both Protestantism and Catholicism are made to dance to Stevens' music.

> Cotton Mather died when I was a boy.
>   The books
> He read, all day, all night and all the
>   nights,
> Had got him nowhere. There was always the
>   doubt,
> That made him preach the louder, long for a
>   church
> In which his voice would roll its cadences,
> After the sermon, to quiet that mouse in
>   the wall.

Protestantism as a moral force, as a force comprehending all of life, never survived the nineteenth century for Stevens. But who is the mysterious mouse? The sermons of Catholicism cannot quiet him.

> Over wooden Boston, the sparking Byzantine
> Was everything that Cotton Mather was
> And more. Yet the eminent thunder from the
>   mouse,
> The grinding in the arches of the church,
> The plaster dropping, even dripping, down,
> The mouse, the moss, the woman on the
>   shore . . . .

The mouse is in the wall working the disintegration of the church. He is associated in Stevens' mind with the natural — "the moss, the woman on the shore." This theme is developed in stanza three.

> If the mouse would swallow the steeple, in
>   its time . . .
> It was a theologian's needle, much
> Too sharp for that. The shore, the sea,
>   the sun,
> The brilliance through the lattices,
>   crippled
> The chandeliers, their morning glazes spread
> In opal blobs along the walls and floor.

The church itself still survives, but is seen to be ineffective in comparison with sea and sun, the natural. Stevens continues:

> Look down, now, Cotton Mather, from the
>   blank.

Equating Heaven with "the blank" is wit that is worthy of the author of "Cortège for Rosenbloom." Still Stevens is willing to make a concession to Mather's imagination, arid though this imagination appears to him.

> Was heaven where you thought? It must
>   be there.

Stevens' own preference for the natural is dominant.

> It must be where you think it is, in the
>   light
> On bed-clothes, in an apple on a plate.
> It is the honey-comb of the seeing man.
> It is the leaf the bird brings back to the
>   boat.

Heaven is where meaning is. Stevens, like Cezanne, can see it in a still-life apple. Or as he puts it more eloquently (and mock-eloquently) in "Academic Discourse at Havana":

> Grandmother and her basketful of pears
> Must be the crux for our compendia.

He can see it in the fulfilled mission of the dove of good tidings. Perhaps, above all, meaning is in the vision of order of the imaginative man. This last explains the title. Many critics have shown that the color blue frequently stands for the imagination and that summer is the season of realization, when the imagination and reality are harmoniously integrated. But summer itself is only one season. Its harmony is no more perdurable than the crystallizations of imaginative vision. The mouse "gets at" summer too. The final stanza shows all systems succumbing to the mouse.

> Go, mouse, go nibble at Lenin in his tomb.
> Are you not le plus pur, you ancient one?
> Cut summer down to find the honey-comb.

You are one . . . Go hunt for honey in his hair.
You are one of the not-numberable mice
Searching all day, all night, for the honey-comb.

Great myths, like Stevens' myth of summer and Lenin's myth of communism, come within the compass of time's bending sickle. Like time, the mouse granulates. It is unappeasable. It is the principle of change in its relentless quest for an order that will be harmonious, for the honey-comb. The mouse is, in Stevens' irreverent view, the power behind the throne, more god than God, the last omnipotence. It is "the eminent thunder" (Stanza II), "le plus pur," the "ancient one," and — parody of holy of holies — "you are one." But it is not the particular mouse itself. Rather it is the quiddity of the mouse that interests Stevens. The mouse is one of a host of "not-numberable mice," a host infinite and omnipresent.

This host has appeared in an earlier poem, "Dance of the Macabre Mice." Here absolute truth, in the form of a statue, a work of art symbolizing the petrification of a once viable myth, is treated indecorously by the unappeasable mice. The mice are called macabre because the imperious statue is not really a statue at all but a skeleton. He is, to quote a line from "Asides on the Oboe," one of

... the metal heroes that time granulates

and as such is a delectable cheese for Stevens' mice. He is absurd in his heroic manner.

The Founder of the State. Whoever founded
A state that was free, in the dead of winter,
    from mice?
What a beautiful tableau tinted and towering
The arm of bronze outstretched against all evil!

It is not that Stevens will not respond to the apotheosis of man, as embodied in the sublimity of the statue. But the statue must be one with the time. Verrocchio in Hartford (there is a pompous equestrian statue of Lafayette in the center of town) just won't do. The statue violates the air. As Stevens says in "Lions in Sweden," if the fault is with the lions, Swenson, send them back to Hamburg. American statues are, or should be, different.

When General Jackson
Posed for his statue
He knew how one feels . . .

. . . . . .

One grows used to the weather,
The landscape and that;
And the sublime comes down
To the spirit itself,

The spirit and space,
The empty spirit
In vacant space.
What wine does one drink?
What bread does one eat?

In this poem, "The American Sublime," the transposition of old to new, religious to secular, pomp to plainness, is implicit. The Christian bread and wine is supplanted by the American sublime which is personal, particular, and disillusioned or without illusion. The words "empty" and "vacant" give the same sense of existential aloneness as "The Snow Man."

But the dominant tone in Stevens' irreverent poems is joy at upsetting the proverbial applecart, in this case, the applecart of old proverbs. Stevens is his own wise man, and worships at his own church.

The lean cats of the arches of the churches,
That's the old world. In the new, all men
    are priests.

("Extracts from Addresses to the Academy of Fine Ideas")

The cats are the old, secretive with the mysteries of religion. They have seen too many lean years. This does not prevent Stevens from treating them in his irreverent manner.

They preach and are preaching in a land
To be described. They are preaching in a time
To be described. Evangelists of what?

The religious cats are ineffectual because, for one thing, there is a fatal lack of unity in their myth.

> If they could gather their theses into one,
> Collect their thoughts together into one,
> Into a single thought, thus: into a queen,
> An intercessor by innate rapport,
> Or into a dark-blue king, *un roi tonnerre,*
> Whose merely being was his valiance,
> Panjandrum and central heart and mind of minds
> If they could!

They obviously cannot, failing to produce a myth that is the center of our being, the imaginative perception of life as we live it. Stevens' sign for this harmonious fusion of imagination and reality is transparence, or the quality that goes with revelation, with lucidity of perception. As he says of the poet, or the imaginative man in each of us (in "Asides on the Oboe"):

> He is the transparence of the place in which
> He is and in his poems we find peace.

Perhaps there is an echo here of Dante's "In his will is our peace." In any case, Stevens does not see this sort of peace existing in organized religion. He sees more muddle than transparence.

> . . . Or is it the multitude of thoughts,
> Like insects in the depths of the mind, that kill
> The single thought? The multitudes of men
> That kill the single man, starvation's head,
> One man, their bread and their remembered wine?
>
> The lean cats of the arches of the churches
> Bask in the sun in which they feel transparent,
> As if designed by X, the per-noble master.

Their apparent transparence is as if designed by X, that unknown missing quantity of deity, that per-noble master, that panjandrum (or, according to the *Oxford Universal Dictionary*, a "nonsense formation . . . . Hence a mock title for a mysterious or an exalted personage; a local magnate of great airs; a pompous pretender"). Such are the "exquisite errors of time," Stevens concludes.

"A High-Toned Old Christian Woman" is another poem which contrasts the old with the new, the moral fictions of religion with the new fictions of poetry. If the opposition between moral law and poetry seems false, it was one that was true for the twenties, when, by virtue of a cultural hyperbole, one was either in the camp of the so-called Puritans and bourgeois or in the camp of the poets and rebels. Stevens makes his preference delightfully clear — delightful to his readers, frightful to the high-toned woman. His tone is even higher.

Poetry is the supreme fiction, madame.

Stevens then contrasts the hymns of "haunted heaven" with the "opposing law," the "bawdiness" of the poets. The old, lean ascetics give way to the men of the new order, the artists. If they too are flagellants, they are a new kind, and hard to tell from clowns.

> Your disaffected flagellants, well-stuffed,
> Smacking their muzzy bellies in parade,
> Proud of such novelties of the sublime,
> Such tink and tank and tunk-a-tunk-tunk,
> May, merely may, madame, whip from themselves
> A jovial hullabaloo among the spheres.
> This will make widows wince. But fictive things
> Wink as they will. Wink most when widows wince.

Here, in all his carefully arranged outrageousness, speaks a champion of the new art. The jovial hullabaloo is to be whipped from man himself and is not to be derived from external agency. This is why the new flagellants are described as disaffected — they are disloyal to the old order and, in that sense evilly affected.

The Puritanism of the Doctor of Geneva (in the poem "The Doctor of Geneva") like that of the high-toned old Christian woman forbids response to things as they are. The "visible, voluble, delugings" of the marvelous Pacific are seen in the mind's eye of the Doctor of Geneva, a son of Calvin, to be "the ruinous waste." This falsification of nature, this disparagement of the sun, Stevens sees as being one step from secular despair. "Gubbinal"[6] is a fine expression of this feeling. Here, the savage sun, the source of energy and creativity, is surrounded by the somberness of a morality which denies that earth is the place for beauty and for happiness.

6. "Gubbins," according to the *OED*, means fragments. If "Gubbinal" is a coinage based on that word, it perhaps refers to the movement of the poem, which is seemingly fragmentary.

> That strange flower, the sun,
> Is just what you say,
> Have it your way.
>
> The world is ugly,
> And the people are sad.
>
> That tuft of jungle feathers,
> That animal eye,
> Is just what you say.
>
> That savage of fire,
> That seed,
> Have it your way.
>
> The world is ugly,
> And the people are sad.

A puritan of nature, Stevens resents the defilement of this intense and austere principle. The "bawdiness" of the new poets is not immorality, but opposition to the severities of Puritan "moral law." Although Stevens shared the dandyism of the early twenties, he is not an aesthete. He may protest against the existing moral order but does not discard the possibility of forming a new one. A moral purpose informs his verse. His bawdiness is nothing more and nothing less than the attempt at a new fiction. Yvor Winters, that high-toned man, cites this poem as evidence of Stevens' incapacity to state his own point of view seriously. Winters seems not at all to suspect that a brilliant clown is most serious when he appears to be least serious. In his essay on Stevens, Winters' critical faculty is blinded by his search for moral absolutes, for universals. Winters envisages a god of reason. But it is precisely this position that Stevens attacks in his assault on deity.

Just as a mud-master was the best Stevens could envisage in the way of deity, so is "The Bird with the Coppery Keen Claws." Here the omnipotent, the omniscient, is seen as an impassive principle of pure intellect.

> Above the forest of the parakeets,
> A parakeet of parakeets prevails . . .
> His lids are white because his eyes are blind.

> He is not paradise of parakeets,
> Of his gold ether, golden alguazil,
> Except because he broods there and is still.
>
> Panache upon panache, his tails deploy
> Upward and outward, in green-vented forms,
> His tip a drop of water full of storms.
>
> But though the turbulent tinges undulate
> As his pure intellect applies its laws,
> He moves not on his coppery, keen claws.

For all his magnificence, the king of the parakeets remains a caricature of a god of reason, an unmoved mover indeed.

Very much in this unflattering vein is the poem "Negation," another description of a blind god. Here God becomes a parody of the idea of omnipotence and omniscience.

> Hi! The creator too is blind,
> Struggling toward his harmonious whole,
> Rejecting intermediate parts,
> Horrors and falsities and wrongs;
> Incapable master of all force,
> Too vague idealist, overwhelmed
> By an afflatus that persists.
> For this, then, we endure brief lives,
> The evanescent symmetries
> From the meticulous potter's thumb.

Stevens defends his position with intelligence. He makes a rational plea for unreason. The antithesis of a poet of an age of reason, say, Pope, he exalts the personal at the expense of the universal.

This, I think, is also the subject of one of Stevens' most discussed poems, "Bantams in Pine-Woods."

> Chieftain Iffucan of Azcan in caftan
> Of tan with henna hackles, halt!
> Damned universal cock, as if the sun
> Was blackamoor to bear your blazing tail.
>
> Fat! Fat! Fat! Fat! I am the personal.
> Your world is you. I am my world.

> You ten-foot poet among inchlings. Fat!
> Begone! An inchling bristles in these pines,
>
> Bristles, and points their Appalachian tangs,
> And fears not portly Azcan nor his hoos.

Chieftain Iffucan is the poet with all the traditional trappings. He is heroic, pompous, official. He is a "damned universal cock," someone standing for the eternal verities. He thinks the sun — Stevens' symbol for the new principle of naturalistic belief — subservient to a moral system. Unconscious of the magnificence of the natural world about him — a fancy rooster dwarfed by immense pines — he is four-times fat, swollen with incongruous pomp. Stevens is the "I," the existential "I," an inchling who claims no special heritage. He is humanity, small basic humanity, small basic embattled humanity, who fears not the voice of priestly authority. Or as Stevens puts it in another poem, "Five Grotesque Pieces" II (*OP*):

> People that live in the biggest houses
> Often have the worst breaths
> Hey-di-ho
>
> The humming bird is the national bird
> Of the humming-bird
> Hey-di-ho.

The man cannot be separated from the mask. That Stevens' hoots and hoos are serious business should be clear by now. That they are comic business should be even more clear. "Bantam in Pine Woods," like the equally famous "The Emperor of Ice-Cream," exhibits pre-eminently what Stevens has called "the essential gaudiness of poetry,"[7] a verbal lavishness and rejoicing which is central to his comic spirit. The more irreverent Stevens becomes the funnier, the better, he becomes. Seldom in modern poetry do we see a poet so obviously enjoying his sense of sheer performance.

The victim of his early satire, in "The Comedian as the Letter C," was romantic illusion. The wit exhibited in the poems of this essay has been at the expense of what Stevens considers outdated myths.

7. Statement by Wallace Stevens, "On the Poem 'Ice Cream' and the 'Meaning' of Poetry," *Explicator*, VII (Nov., 1948), 18.

In very different essays, Hi Simons[8] and Stanley Burnshaw[9] writing about the line in "The Comedian" — "For realist, what is is what should be" — say that Stevens is making the Popean assertion, "Whatever is, is right." Neither critic does justice to either Pope or Stevens. When Pope says "Whatever is, is right" he is thinking, with tempered optimism, in terms of the great chain of being set infallibly down from heaven by God almighty — or a rational facsimile thereof. Pope was perhaps the last great poet to think in these terms, terms which were very meaningful to Milton and Shakespeare. But Stevens, a modern, cannot reason about the universe with such assurance. It is not so much a matter of a chain of being as a thread of becoming. Both seek an idea of order. By order both meant a control of chaos; but where Pope thinks of order in terms of universal degree, Stevens thinks of order in terms of the imaginative comprehension of reality, a reality which is no less illusive for being actuality. This is what he means by "For realist, what is is what should be." When Stevens seems to be making concessions to a deistic universe, he is really doing the irreverent opposite.

> If there must be a god in the house, must be,
> Saying things in the rooms and on the stair,
>
> Let him move as the sunlight moves on the floor,
> Or moonlight, silently, as Plato's ghost
>
> Or Aristotle's skeleton. Let him hang out
> His stars on the wall. He must dwell quietly.
>
> He must be incapable of speaking. . . .

Part of the ridicule here is made by the juxtaposition of the supposedly ethereal god with mundane objects of our real world like rooms and stairs. Plato and Aristotle, both shadows of themselves for Stevens, represented as they are by a ghost and a skeleton, have at least the virtue of making no claims for a personalized deity. The poem is called "Less and Less Human O Savage Spirit." The title refers to the nature of the universe as it appears to Stevens. The fiction of a personal deity violates Stevens' sense of man's isolation in the universe.

8. Hi Simons, "The Comedian as the Letter C," *Southern Review*, V (Winter, 1940), 464.
9. Stanley Burnshaw, Review of *Ideas of Order*, by Wallace Stevens, *New Masses*, XVII (Oct. 1, 1935), 41 f.

> It is the human that is the alien,
> The human that has no cousin in the moon.
> . . . .
>
> If there must be a god in the house, let him be one
> That will not hear us when we speak: a coolness,
>
> A vermilioned nothingness, any stick of the mass
> Of which we are too distantly a part.

The sense of existential alienation is not *the* tone of Stevens' poetry about life as lived on earth. Equally characteristic, as we have seen in "Ploughing on Sunday," is the exhilaration of living. The last disillusionment with outdated mythology does not always leave the realist shaken or even alone. As we switch from old to new marvelous things can happen — and do in a poem appropriately called "The Sense of the Sleight of Hand Man." It begins with the typically indecorous Stevens wit.

> One's grand flights, one's Sunday baths,
> One's tootings at the weddings of the soul
> Occur as they occur.

Here wading in religiosity is given its satiric recompense. "Sunday baths" is marvelous. It is the keynote of the grandiosity of the first stanza which is a description of the windy, the cloudy, the empty — in short, the old belief. But the wheel of fortune, here seen as the wheel of nature, creates a new reality and presto:

> Could you have said the bluejay suddenly
> Would swoop to earth? It is a wheel, the rays
> Around the sun. The wheel survives the myths.
> The fire eye in the clouds survives the gods.

The description of the sun is reminiscent of the description of it in "Gubbinal." There is the same sense of savage energy. But the sleight-of-hand man has more tricks.

> To think of a dove with an eye of grenadine
> And pines that are cornets, so it occurs . . . .

And finally, the stellar feat.

> And a little island full of geese and stars.

The last vision is charming in its naiveté; but it is a naiveté achieved, not a naiveté born. But Stevens has a warm feeling for the latter as well. The poet shares with the ignorant man a free and intuitive response to reality.

> It may be that the ignorant man, alone,
> Has any chance to mate his life with life
> That is the sensual, pearly spouse, the life
> That is fluent in even the wintriest bronze.

Even the most sober disillusioned thought, "the wintriest bronze," cannot dispel the charm of natural beauty.

Stevens is an earth-intoxicated man; even in the chaotic 1930's this love sustained him.

> Marx has ruined Nature,
> For the moment . . .
>
>   .   .   .   .   .   .
>
> The pillars are prostrate, the arches
>   are haggard,
> The hotel is boarded and bare.
> Yet the panorama of despair
> Cannot be the specialty
> Of this ecstatic air.
>
> ("Botanist on Alp No. I")

Although Stevens will not be remembered for his political views, it is important to notice the effect the political ferment of the 1930's had on the nature-minded iconoclast. We may see this effect in a poem like "Sad Strains of a Gay Waltz," a "political" poem which is cast in the rhetoric of irreverence:

> The truth is that there comes a time
> When we can mourn no more over music
> That is so much motionless sound.
>
> There comes a time when the waltz
> Is no longer a mode of desire, a mode
> Of revealing desire and is empty of shadows.
>
> Too many waltzes have ended.

The once renowned music of the spheres is now motionless sound. The view of universal harmony that could motivate the metaphor, say, in Sir John Davies' "Orchestra," of the cosmic order being a measured, ordered, dance, a waltz, is now ended. The music of the waltz is now sad; it is the last waltz to be heard. After this passage there comes what seems at first a curious digression.

> . . . And then
> There's that mountain-minded Hoon,
> For whom desire was never that of the waltz,
> Who found all form and order in solitude,
> For whom the shapes were never the figures of men.
> Now, for him, his forms have vanished.
> There is order in neither sea nor sun.
> The shapes have lost their glistening.
> There are these sudden mobs of men. . . .

Who is this Hoon? We know that he never liked the old order or waltzes. We know that he has a preference for sea and sun over men, and that he is a solitary figure. All of which leads us to believe that Hoon is, in this poem, a self-ironic projection of Stevens, whose remoteness was legendary and who said of himself — "Life is an affair of people not of places. But for me life is an affair of places and that is the trouble" (*Adagia*). Furthermore, if we look at a poem in *Harmonium* called "Tea at the Palace of Hoon," we see what is obviously a projection of Stevens. Here again Stevens uses religious props, hymns and holy water, in a secular way.

> Not less because in purple I descended
> The western day through what you called
> The loneliest air, not less was I myself.
>
> What was the ointment sprinkled on my beard?
> What were the hymns that buzzed beside my ears?
> What was the sea whose tide swept through me there?
>
> Out of my mind the golden ointment rained,
> And my ears made the blowing hymns they heard.
> I was myself the compass of that sea:
>
> I was the world in which I walked, and what I saw

> Or heard or felt came not but from myself;
> And there I found myself more truly and more strange.

Hoon is plainly the imaginative man who can supply a mythology of self. The language and sentiment in the last four lines is close to that of "The Idea of Order at Key West," where it is poetry itself creating mythology. In "Tea" the image of Hoon is heroic; but the thirties made Stevens doubt this image of himself, as mythology of self seemed to be obscured by

> These sudden clouds of faces and arms; . . .
> Requiring order beyond their speech.

> Too many waltzes have ended. Yet the shapes
> For which the voices cry, these, too, may be
> Modes of desire, modes of revealing desire.

> > ("Sad Strains of a Gay Waltz")

The new modes of desire arising from the social chaos are associated with the end of the old music. The new myth will be instrumental in dispelling the political chaos.

> Too many waltzes — the epic of disbelief
> Blares oftener and soon, will soon be constant.
> Some harmonious skeptic soon in a skeptical music

> Will unite these figures of men and their shapes
> Will glisten again with motion, the music
> Will be motion and full of shadows.

Stevens sees the new order as skeptical, as doubting the validity of theological truth and the social systems it has helped to support. The skepticism has a music, or a mythology forged out of art, of its own. "The relation of art to life is of the first importance especially in a skeptical age," says Stevens in the *Adagia*, "since in the absence of a belief in God, the mind turns to its own creations and examines them, not alone from the aesthetic point of view, but for what they reveal, for what they validate and invalidate, for the support that they give."

Stevens' attempt to bring man to an understanding of existence, his attempt to gratify some of the demands of humanity that religion had too successfully exorcised, together with his need to find a way out of the old rhetoric, are a measure of his sympathy with the French poets of the latter half of the nineteenth century. Stevens, of Pennsylvania Dutch ancestry, explains this to a revered Teutonic ancestor, in the poem called "Explanation."

> Ach, Mutter,
> This old, black dress,
> I have been embroidering
> French flowers on it.
>
> Not by way of romance,
> Here is nothing of the ideal,
> Nein,
> Nein.
>
> It would have been different,
> Liebchen,
> If I had imagined myself,
> In an orange gown,
> Drifting through space,
> Like a figure on the church-wall.

Had Stevens stuck to the old pieties he might have written something worthy of the figure on the façade of a German cathedral. Stevens makes the statement with some filial nostalgia for the old. But he remains a hard-headed Dutchman, true to his skeptical bias. Because of this Stevens can hope that

> . . . the world is averted
> From an old delusion, an old affair with the
>   sun,
> An impossible aberration with the moon,
> A grossness of peace.
>
> It is not the snow that is the quill, the page.
> The poem lashes more fiercely than the wind,
> As the mind, to find what will suffice, destroys
> Romantic tenements of rose and ice.

The word "romantic" here, as in "Explanation," has the force of sentimental. The name of the poem is "Man and Bottle." The title seems to imply that this courageous assertion must be sustained by spirits at times, but earthly ones to be sure.

It takes courage to declare one's independence, to declare that being is the conclusion of all appearances.

> Let be be finale of seem
> The only emperor is the emperor of ice-cream . . .
> Let the lamp affix its beam
> The only emperor is the emperor of ice-cream.

This famous refrain from the much-expounded poem, "The Emperor of Ice-Cream," expresses Stevens' credo. Reduced to a paraphrase it is this: the magnificence we can achieve in our human state, which is delicious but does not last forever, is the only magnificence; therefore, let us see things the way they really are. As with "Bantams in Pine-Woods," Stevens makes this poem ring with his celebrated flamboyance, with the essential gaudiness of poetry. As Richard Ellman says, this poem shows the right way to conduct a funeral.[10] This statement is, of course, an hyperbole; but the point is that we should not be intimidated by death, that the laws of irreverence can be the laws of freedom. The old fictions must be seen to be expendable.

> The prologues are over. It is a question, now,
> Of final belief. So, say that final belief
> Must be in fiction. It is time to choose.

> That obsolete fiction of the wide river in
> An empty land; the gods that Boucher killed;
> And the metal heroes that time granulates —
> The philosophers' man alone still walks in dew,
> Still by the sea-side mutters milky lines
> Concerning an immaculate imagery.

("Asides on the Oboe")

The "wide river" seems to be an allusion to the drowning of the Egyptian hordes; the reference to Boucher, Hi Simons tells us, is to the anthropomorphic mythologies which have been rationalized since the eighteenth century;[11] the "metal heroes" are things like the lions in Sweden or a Verrocchio man on horse. Still, the philosophers' man

---

10. Richard Ellmann, "Wallace Stevens' 'Ice-Cream' " *Kenyon Review*, XIX (Winter, 1957), 92.

11. Hi Simons, "The Genre of Wallace Stevens," *Sewanee Review*, LIII (Autumn, 1945), 570.

builds a myth through his own immaculate conceptions. This culture hero is described as

> The impossible possible philosophers' man

because the new fiction he creates makes what once seemed impossible, possible. He creates new possibilities. He is

> The man who has had the time to think enough
> The central man, the human globe, responsive
> As a mirror with a voice, the man of glass,
> Who in a million diamonds sums us up.

"Central" is Stevens' word for the fusion of imagination and reality. The central man is a globe, a mirror, a man of glass because he shows things the way they really are, in his articulate and brilliant crystallization of vision. He is not the alienated poet as much as he is the best expression of human consciousness. Stevens knows that in our time it is difficult to conceive the poet as hero.

> The poet striding among the cigar stores,
> Ryan's lunch, hatters, insurance and
>   medicines . . . .

Nevertheless he must have a vision, he

> Denies that abstraction is a vice except
> To the fatuous . . .
> One man, the idea of man, that is the space,
> The true abstract in which he promenades.
> The era of the idea of man, the cloak
> And speech of Virgil dropped, that's where he
>   walks,
> That's where his hymns come crowding, hero-
>   hymns,
> Chorals for mountain voices and the moral
>   chant,
> Happy rather than holy but happy-high,
> Day hymns instead of constellated rhymes,
> Hymns of the struggle of the idea of god
> And the idea of man . . . .
>
>   ("A Thought Revolved" II)

The poet imagines an image of man, not with any historical Vergilian sense of mission, but merely as wholly human; indeed he imagines a new fiction emerging from the conflict between personal and idealistic views of experience. Stevens believes with religious ardor in his homey hero, and in his heroic home. His elegiac feeling for the natural world is one with his sweet perception of natural man. In our time when, if there is a God, he has become increasingly difficult to know, Stevens' reverence for what we do know contains more piety than the dogmas of the contradictory creeds which claim to know the answers. The general violence of the world being what it now is, can we say more than "God is in me or else is not at all (does not exist)" — as Stevens says in his *Adagia*. Stevens' poetry points to the fact that there is more piety in being human than in being pious. His irreverence is sacred. He wants nothing less holy than the oneness of man and his world. Almost too many claims have been made for absolute truth for man to see his natural, beautiful, and rightful inheritance.

> It was when I said,
> "There is no such thing as the truth,"
> That the grapes seemed fatter.
> The fox ran out of his hole.
>
> You . . . you said,
> "There are many truths,
> But they are not parts of a truth."
> Then the tree, at night, began to change,
>
> Smoking through green and smoking blue.
> We were two figures in a wood.
> We said we stood alone.
>
> It was when I said,
> "Words are not forms of a single word.
> In the sum of the parts, there are only the parts.
> The world must be measured by eye";
>
> It was when you said,
> "The idols have seen lots of poverty,
> Snakes and gold and lice,
> But not the truth";

> It was at that time, that the silence was
>   largest
> And longest, the night was roundest,
> The fragrance of the autumn warmest,
> Closest and strongest.

> ("On the Road Home")

Chapter 4: "This Venerable Complication"

*A*n iconoclast, upon being asked what he proposed to set up in place of the things he had been tearing down, replied that it was difficult enough to assault obsolete values with courage and effectiveness and that he never really gave any thought to expounding any values of his own. Wallace Stevens is in the perhaps less enviable position of having values of his own, which may be challenged as spiritedly as those he has challenged. The image of Stevens as a poet who does not seriously represent a point of view, who succeeds only in representing a tableau of exquisite sensations, is no longer put forth. There is, in fact, agreement as to what is central in his point of view. A central theme, the theme which will concern us in this chapter, is one he vexes from early poetry to late, the relation of imagination to reality. What this relationship is, however, has not been a subject of agreement. An understanding of his comic spirit takes us to the core of his position.

Stevens' prose, which usually explores this relationship with an explicitness not always present in his poetry, may serve as a beginning. In his essay "The Figure of the Youth as Virile Poet" the youth, who represents imagination and is therefore a persona for Stevens, says: *"I am the truth, since I am part of what is real, but neither more nor less than those around me. And I am imagination, in a leaden time and in a world that does not move for the weight of its own heaviness."*[1] The youth is saying, first, that the imagination is a reality, in that it is a fact, a fact which is no more nor less real than social reality or "the life that is lived in the scene that it composes."[2] He is also saying that it is very hard for him since the social reality is in its heavy, intractable way a challenge to his existence. Stevens, being an insurance executive as well as a poet, is, perhaps, especially qualified to comment on this scene. But his view of the common life is not so complimentary as his view of poetry. When Stevens, in a magazine interview, was asked, "As a poet what distinguishes you, do you think, from an ordinary man?" he replied, " . . . inability to see much point to the life of an ordinary man. The chances are an ordinary man himself sees very little point to it."[3] Or, when questioned about the condition of American labor, he vigorously admits his indifference to the subject: "I suppose . . . I am against the CIO and for the AF of L. But this is all most incidental with me and rather a ridiculous thing for me to be talking about. My direct interests are with something quite different. My direct interest is in telling the archbishop of Canterbury to go jump off the end of the dock."[4] Stevens' apparent coming to terms with ordinary life in his capacity as an insurance executive is much more a matter of the attractions of a business life than a sense of community. Like the figure of the youth he has no trouble in conceiving social reality as a dull burden.

In "The Common Life" Stevens paints a bleak landscape.

> That's the down-town frieze,
> Principally the church steeple,
> A black line beside a white line;

1. Wallace Stevens, *The Necessary Angel* (New York: Alfred A. Knopf, 1951), p. 63. Hereafter, I will refer to Stevens' book of essays as *NA*.
2. *Ibid.*, p. 25.
3. Reply to questionnaire of Geoffrey Grigson, *New Verse*, XI (Oct., 1934), 2, 15.
4. In a letter to Hi Simons dated Jan. 12, 1940.

And the stack of the electric plant,
A black line drawn on flat air.

It is a morbid light
In which they stand,
Like an electric lamp
On a page of Euclid.

In this light a man is a result,
A demonstration, and a woman,
Without rose and without violet,
The shadows that are absent from Euclid,
Is not a woman for a man.

The common life, usually having the virtues of sensuousness, is here seen as bloodless, sexless, a function of the mechanized abstraction of modern industrial society, a rational catastrophe. We are in the two-dimensional realm of absolute fact. The only color is a contrast in colorlessness. What is lacking is imaginative life.

The paper is whiter
For these black lines.
It glares beneath the webs
Of wire, the designs of ink,
The planes that ought to have genius,
The volumes like marble ruins
Outlined and have alphabetical
Notations and footnotes.
The paper is whiter.
The men have no shadows
And the women have only one side.

Wistfully, an image of learning and myth is evoked, the three-dimensionality of which is insisted upon. The condition here, however somberly set forth, is ameliorated by the vivid caricature of it.

The stale atmosphere of unmitigated colorlessness is the theme of one of Stevens' most high-spirited satiric poems, "Disillusionment of Ten O'Clock." The preposition "of" rather than "at" in the title indicates that this is a periodic occurrence, not merely an isolated event. As in "The Common Life" a dull whiteness saturates the air.

> The houses are haunted
> By white night-gowns
> None are green,
> Or purple with green rings,
> Or green with yellow rings,
> Or yellow with blue rings.
> None of them are strange,
> With socks of lace
> And beaded ceintures.
> People are not going
> To dream of baboons and periwinkles.
> Only, here and there, an old sailor,
> Drunk and asleep in his boots,
> Catches tigers
> In red weather.

The houses are "haunted" because colorless uniformity has made people ghosts of themselves. There is no exotic display of color in the houses, there are no daring dreams. Only the old sailor (presumably related to the mock-heroic skinny sailor peering through the sea-glass of "The Comedian as the Letter C," who is a comic projection of Stevens) achieves the intensity of remote, heroic action as he dreams in the imaginative intensity of red. Glossing this poem leaves much unsaid. It is obvious that the tone of Stevens' comedy is defined by statements of fantasy as well as statements of rationality, play mixed with what Freud calls tendency wit, nonsense with sociology. Nevertheless, the psychological origin or meeting ground of image and idea can be perceived.

Sometimes an ordinary life is enlivened by a dreamlike interlude of imaginative fruition. "The Ordinary Women" is a poem which shows what happens when people in white nightgowns do dream of periwinkles.

> Then from their poverty they rose,
> From dry catarrhs, and to guitars
> They flitted
> Through the palace walls.

> They flung monotony behind,
> Turned from their want, and, nonchalant,
> They crowded
> The nocturnal halls.
>
> The lacquered loges huddled there
> Mumbled zay-zay and a-zay, a-zay,
> The moonlight
> Fubbed the girandoles.

The women rise from the poverty of the ordinary, symbolized by dry catarrhs, to the exoticism of the imaginative, symbolized by the guitars. The mandarin language supports the dramatic situation, underscoring the exoticism of the new scene. Indeed, the mandarin language is in one sense the dramatic situation, since this is one of the numerous poems of Stevens whose meaning resides as much in the way words are used as in any gloss. The poem is motivated by an impulse toward elegant improvisation, a delight in displaying the refined for its own sake which is, psychologically, inseparable from Stevens' awareness of the rarity of this delight in a society where the extraordinary seems to be difficult to locate. (But does not the language become excessively fine? For example, "The moonlight/ Fubbed the girandoles" is perhaps too difficult to paraphrase — assuming that sooner or later that is one of the necessary aspects of reading poetry — the moonlight evaded the chandeliers or cheated them in being brighter. Nevertheless, the fact that Stevens uses such words has a meaning which is clear enough.)

In this atmosphere of moonlit revery, the peculiar charm of the imagination becomes clear. It enhances, clarifies, exalts, mingling with intense desire.

> And the cold dresses that they wore,
> In the vapid haze of the window-bays,
> Were tranquil
> As they leaned and looked
>
> From the window-sills at the alphabets,
> At beta b and gamma g,
> To study
> The canting curlicues

Of heaven and of the heavenly script.
And there they read of marriage-bed
Ti-lill-o!
And they read right long.

The gaunt guitarists on the strings
Rumbled a-day and a-day, a-day.
The moonlight
Rose on the beachy floors.

How explicit the coiffures became.
The diamond point, the sapphire point,
The sequins
Of the civil fans!

Imaginatively perceived, things become more meaningful; the stories
they read add excitement to their lives. Similarly, the coiffures of the
women become explicit in the light of the imagination. But the ladies
are ordinary after all, and for all they read of marriage-bed, they are
afraid of their desire. Their imaginations are too active for them, and
they return to the world of throat ailments.

Insinuations of desire,
Puissant speech, alike in each,
Cried quittance
To the wickless halls.

Then from their poverty they rose,
From dry guitars, and to catarrhs
They flitted
Through the palace walls.

They are truly poor in that they do not heed the insinuations of
desire. This is what cries quittance to the imaginative escapade.

"Loneliness in Jersey City" shows another tableau of social reality
as boredom. Natural grace, represented by the deer, is indistinguish-
able from domestic unseemliness, represented by the dachshund. The
ordinary animals have cause for jubilation.

Kiss, cats: for the deer and the dachshund
Are one. My window is twenty-nine three
And plenty of window for me.
The steeples are empty and so are the
people,

> There's nothing whatever to see
> Except Polaks that pass in their motors
> And play concertinas all night,
> They think that things are all right,
> Since the deer and the dachshund are one.

Aside from motoring and the minstrelsy of concertinas (echoed in the singsong verse), the only activity on the horizon is window-watching. Such is life in Jersey City.

After such knowledge, what forgiveness? The imaginative man is at best in this company a solitary singer, or his pharynx may fail altogether and the poet may be mute. This is the situation of "The Man Whose Pharynx Was Bad." Here the poet has succumbed to what Stevens calls "the pressure of reality." By this phrase he means "the pressure of an external event or events on the consciousness to the exclusion of any power of contemplation."[5] The dullness of everyday reality has depressed the poet in this poem which Marius Bewley rightly compares to Coleridge's "Ode to Dejection."[6] In both poems the subject is a failure of imagination and the exploration of a new emotion which arises from this incapacity. But where Coleridge can write in majestic terms, indeed write even an exalted ode, about his condition, Stevens must self-ironically call his condition by a name that will elicit the sympathy of those around him. Where Coleridge can use the intimacy of first person confession, Stevens must mute his complaint by referring to himself in the anonymous third person, as the man whose pharynx was bad.

> The time of year has grown indifferent.
> Mildew of summer and the deepening snow
> Are both alike in the routine I know.
> I am too dumbly in my being pent.
>
> The wind attendant on the solstices
> Blows on the shutters of the metropoles,
> Stirring no poet in his sleep, and tolls
> The grand ideas of the villages.

5. NA, p. 20.
6. Marius Bewley, "The Poetry of Wallace Stevens," *Partisan Review*, XVI (Sept., 1949), 909 f.

The power of the poet's imagination is dissipated before the depressing flux of daily routine. He makes no distinction between snowy winter (in Stevens' private mythology this is the time when things are seen clearly and stripped of false illusion, the first step toward conceiving reality imaginatively) and summer (or the time when imagination and reality are one). He thinks wishfully of the proper climate of imagination.

> The malady of the quotidian . . .
> Perhaps if summer ever came to rest[7]
> And lengthened, deepened, comforted,
>   caressed
> Through days like oceans in obsidian
>
> Horizons, full of night's midsummer blaze
> Perhaps, if winter once could penetrate
> Through all its purples to the final slate,
> Persisting bleakly in an icy haze,
>
> One might in turn become less diffident,
> Out of such mildew plucking neater mould
> And spouting new orations of the cold.
> One might. One might. But time will not
>   relent.

Imaginative fruition and the power of honest disillusion are forgotten in the flux of the relentless quotidian routine. Under the pressure of reality summer remains mildew and the mind of winter cannot penetrate to the universal hue of the sky, to life's natural *donné*, to the substance in us that prevails.

Stifling though the malady of the quotidian may be, Stevens does not remain discouraged. He is not one to save the imagination by escaping reality. When he says that "the imagination has the strength of reality or none at all," he is saying that reality is to be mastered by the imagination as well as endured. Even though modern man may be typified by the figure of a man putting up telephone poles in a suburb whose air is saturated by various industrial oxides, the imaginative man must not evade this reality. He must create a myth out of what he beholds.

7. Bewley rightly laments the deletion, in the *Collected Poems*, of the four lines which follow. See Bewley, *ibid.*, 908 ff.

> At last, in spite of his manner, his eye
>
> A-cock at the cross-piece on a pole
> Supporting heavy cables, slung
>
> Through Oxidia, banal suburb,
> One-half of all its installments paid.
>
> Dew-dapper clapper-traps, blazing
> From crusty stacks above machines.
>
> Ecce, Oxidia is the seed
> Dropped out of this amber-ember pod,
>
> Oxidia is the soot of fire,
> Oxidia is Olympia.
>
> ("Man with the Blue Guitar" XXX)

Commenting on this passage Stevens says, "The necessity is to evolve a man from modern life — from Oxidia, not Olympia, since Oxidia is our only Olympia."[8]

Creating a myth for Oxidia is a tenuous occupation. In the early poem "The Plot against the Giant," reality emerges as something gross and slovenly, as monstrous actuality, or so it seems in the view of an excessively fastidious aestheticism. Three young lady aesthetes cannot see reality for the refinements they would make of it.

> *First Girl*
> When this yokel comes maundering,
> Whetting his hacker,
> I shall run before him,
> Diffusing the civilest odors
> Out of geraniums and unsmelled flowers.
> It will check him.

Reality is simple, unadorned, arrant and a big problem. The offended girls are out to transform their crude acquaintance. The first, by delicate scent; the second, by exquisite color.

> *Second Girl*
> I shall run before him,
> Arching clothes besprinkled with colors

8. *Mattino Domenicale*, p. 182.

As small as fish-eggs.
The threads
Will abash him.

It is the third girl who delivers the *coup de grace*. She pities him.

> *Third Girl*
> Oh, la . . . le pauvre!
> I shall run before him,
> With a curious puffing.
> He will bend his ear then.
> I shall whisper
> Heavenly labials in a world of gutturals.
> It will undo him.

She would transform the discord of reality by a harmonious but rare-fied speech. It may seem that this is very much what Stevens himself is trying to do, lend grace to the ugly, color to the colorless. But it seems to me that Sevens is engaging in a self caricature of his early tendency toward aestheticism. We do not see reality here through the eyes of Stevens, but from the point of view of excessively fastidious aesthetes. How differently this aspect of reality is perceived by a true persona of Stevens in "The Comedian as the Letter C." Like Crispin, Stevens is not the one to deny or shrink from the guttural aspects of life. He is as aware of the unseemliness of reality as he is of its seduc-tiveness. "There is an intensely pejorative aspect of the idea of the real," says Stevens in *Adagia*. "The opposite should be the case. Its own poetry is actual." The aesthetes, no less than the rationalists and the religious orthodox, oversimplify and distort the relation of imagina-tion to reality. They are sentimental about reality, and are hence un-wittingly sentimental about the imagination. In trying to purge the unbeautiful from the world they are relegating the imagination to an all too ethereal role which Stevens would not like to see it possess. Stevens never claims that the imagination is a faculty which lives in independent exquisiteness and divine loneliness.

One may be too literally a realist of the imagination. The everyday realities must not be forgotten. "A Rabbit as King of Ghosts" shows how living in imagination alone is a kind of hallucination. The word "ghosts" in the title indicates that Stevens will depict a caricature of idealism, the exclusive idealism which Stevens is perpetually assault-

ing. There is a similar undercutting of idealism in the first lines of
"The Comedian as the Letter C."

> Nota: man is the intelligence of his soil,
> The sovereign ghost.

Like the lowly young Crispin, the common rabbit is a victim of the
falsifying power of imagination. Like the typically imaginative man,
the rabbit works by night in arduous contemplation.

> The difficulty to think at the end of day,
> When the shapeless shadow covers the sun
> And nothing is left except light on your fur . . . .

In contrast to this, we are offered a picture of colorful daylight actuality. It is bright day in the most summery month.

> There was the cat slopping its milk all day,
> Fat cat, red tongue, green mind, white milk
> And August the most peaceful month.

The thoughtful rabbit, nightdweller, does not contemplate this actuality with delight. Rather, he feels the cat an antagonistic element,
immovable but something he would like to remove.

> To be, in the grass, in the peacefullest time,
> Without that monument of cat,
> The cat forgotten in the moon . . . .

The rabbit would like to forget the cat, he would wish reality to be
forgotten in the moon, in the benign light of the imagination. As in
"The Comedian as the Letter C," "Men Made Out of Words" (in
which Stevens chastises "castratos of moonmash"), and other poems,
the moon is made to represent an imagination which is not always
elevating or an imagination which inflates rather than exalts. Free
of the conditions of the real, one feels a clinical euphoria:

> And to feel that the light is a rabbit-light,
> In which everything is meant for you
> And nothing need be explained;

> Then there is nothing to think of. It comes of itself;
> And east rushes west and west rushes down,
> No matter. The grass is full

> And full of yourself. The trees around are for you,
> The whole of the wideness of night is for you,
> A self that touches all edges,
>
> You become a self that fills the four corners of night.
> The red cat hides away in the fur-light
> And there you are humped high, humped up,
>
> You are humped higher and higher, black as stone —
> You sit with your head like a carving in space
> And the little green cat is a bug in the grass.

The rabbit is indeed a sovereign ghost, the master of an all too spiritual reality. Being a king of ghosts, he is a ghost himself. He is the caricature of the poet as powerhouse; "the monument of cat" has been usurped by the rabbit which is "humped higher and higher black as stone . . . like a carving in space." Reality has been reduced to a figment of the imagination, as imagination is reduced to a caricature of itself. For Stevens the true imagination is the highest form of consciousness, a conjunction of desire and conception which acts on the actual world — that is, man in society and physical nature. Stevens equates being good with being aware, steering a middle course between the literalness of the unimaginative rationalist and the exaltation of the uninspired idealist. He is as wary of the vague romantic (in a pejorative sense) as he is of the limitations of the ascetic reason. Both obscure the possibility of our seeing things the way they are. Here is Stevens steering his course through this Scylla and Charybdis in the essay called "Imagination as Value."

. . . we must somehow cleanse the imagination of the romantic. We feel, without being particularly intelligent about it, that the imagination as metaphysics will survive logical positivism unscathed. At the same time, we feel, and with the sharpest possible intelligence, that it is not worthy to survive if it is to be identified with the romantic. The imagination is one of the great human powers. The romantic belittles it. The imagination is the liberty of the mind. The romantic is a failure to make use of that liberty. It is a failure of the imagination precisely as sentimentality is a failure of feeling. The imagination is the only genius. It is intrepid and eager and the extreme of its achievement lies in abstraction. The achievement of the romantic, on the contrary, lies in minor wish-fulfillments and it is incapable of abstraction.[9]

9. *NA*, p. 138.

The romantic-sentimental fosters a too easy identification between imagination and reality, preferring an ideal world to the real one.

In the other, the good sense of the word, Stevens is himself a romantic, himself a chauvinist of the self. It was the romantics who proclaimed their faith in the sustaining and ennobling power of the imagination and in the reality of the natural world. It was the romantics too who sought a oneness between man and the natural world, making knowledge something real rather than something certain. Although Stevens shares these qualities with some of the English romantic poets, he is wary of attributing too much felicity to nature. More than this, Stevens is as sensitive to the excesses of the imagination as he is to its virtues. Sentimental and clichéd language is the indication of an imagination gone stale. This can be as fatal an enemy to the true perception of reality as outmoded belief. It is, in fact, a kind of outmoded belief. It is, therefore, choice material for Stevens' deflationary wit.

> A very felicitous eve,
> Herr Doktor, and that's enough,
> Though the brow in your palm may grieve
>
> At the vernacular of light
> (Omitting reefs of cloud);
> Empurpled garden grass;
>
> The spruces' outstretched hands;
> The twilight overfull
> Of wormy metaphors.
>
> ("Delightful Evening")

Stevens would recognize the felicity in nature but let the romantic sentimentality go. For "Herr Doktor," perhaps a German transcendentalist, the twilight calls forth purple rhetoric which is downright awful. His metaphors are wormy because they come from a poetic corpse, a language which is dead for Stevens. The modest title, "Delightful Evening," further contrasts Stevens' sense of the experience with that of the Doktor. The Doktor, like the three aesthetes in "The Plot against the Giant," in the guise of imagination is really belittling imagination. Substituting wish-fulfillment for the daring which is its native element, the imagination becomes a merely sentimental faculty.

The girl who would whisper heavenly labials in a world of gutturals and the Doktor who emotes about the "spruces' outstretched hands" are poetic in the bad sense. They are like the poet who writes an effete poetry of sheer sound — a caricature of feeling and imagination. The imagination does not meet the challenge of reality. "The Creations of Sound" is another caricature of the romantic as sentimental.

> If the poetry of X was music,
> So that it came to him of its own,
> Without understanding, out of the wall
>
> Or in the ceiling, in sounds not chosen,
> Or chosen quickly, in a freedom
> That was their element, we should not know
>
> That X is an obstruction, a man
> Too exactly himself, and that there are words
> Better without an author, without a poet,
>
> Or having a separate author, a different poet,
> An accretion from ourselves, intelligent
> Beyond intelligence, an artificial man
>
> At a distance, a secondary expositor,
> A being of sound, whom one does not approach
> Through any exaggeration. From him, we
>   collect.

This difficult poem seems to say that the poet who writes a poetry of sound without some organized principle of meaning is no poet but poetic in the bad sense; that poetry is not the poetical, but the imaginative expression of the intelligence beyond intelligence, the intuitive in man. Poetry, Stevens maintains well after *Harmonium*, is not a matter of exaggerated sound effects. The poet of sound is an "obstruction, a man/ Too exactly himself." He relies too literally on his senses and not on the "accretion from ourselves, intelligent beyond intelligence." We do not know that X is an obstruction because we are enchanted by the music. The trouble with X is, that like the girl who would whisper heavenly labials in a world of gutturals, his tastes would refine things beyond the point of reality. He is ethereal, but this is not what is wanted. Like the three aesthete girls and Herr Doktor, X obscures reality by doing nothing more than making it pretty.

> Tell X that speech is not dirty silence
> Clarified. It is silence made still dirtier.
> It is more than an imitation for the ear.
>
> He lacks this venerable complication.
> His poems are not of the second part of life.
> They do not make the visible a little hard
>
> To see . . . .

The silence of the world of gutturals must not be made pretty, but must be complicated by a denser silence which is the imaginative confrontation of this reality. This is "more than an imitation for the ear." This is the "venerable complication." Stevens' poetry is part of the second part of life, is part of the imaginative complication. Stevens concludes,

> We say ourselves in syllables that rise
> From the floor.

His foundation is always earthly, as opposed to the poet of sound whose apparently elevated music comes to him

> . . . out of the wall
> Or in the ceiling . . . .

Clearly he aspires too high.

Despite this denigration of the romantic, Stevens considers himself a romantic. He has a sense of what has become obsolete in the romantic and what has not. He therefore is very sensitive to the pejorative use of the word, a use which he finds sometimes necessary and sometimes irritating. "It should be said of poetry that it is essentially romantic," says Stevens in *Adagia*, "as if one were recognizing the truth about poetry for the first time. Although the romantic is referred to most often in a pejorative sense, this sense attaches, or should attach, not to the romantic in general but to some phase of the romantic which has become stale. Just as there is always a romantic that is potent, so there is always a romantic that is impotent." Stevens has dealt with great wit about some of the outdated aspects of the romantic. But he himself is the first to exalt the imaginative and intuitive rather than the logical and rational, the poetic rather than the philosophic. Stevens openly identifies himself with the romantic that he considers potent. "The imaginative is the romantic" he says in *Adagia*. He states his case more specifically in a brief essay on the poetry of Marianne Moore:

The romantic in the pejorative sense merely connotes obsolescence, but that word has, or should have, another sense . . . [The] romantic in its other sense, meaning always the living and at the same time the imaginative, the youthful, the delicate and a variety of things which it is not necessary to try to particularize at the moment, constitutes the vital element in poetry. It is absurd to wince at being called a romantic poet. Unless one is that one is not a poet at all. That, of course, does not meant banyans and frangipani; and it cannot for long mean no banyans and no frangipani. Just what it means Miss Moore's book discloses. It means, now-a-days, an uncommon intelligence. It means in a time like our own of violent feelings equally violent feelings and the most skilfull expression of the genuine.[10]

Stevens' sense of the romantic is general, indicating a certain imaginative intensity and daring. Just how general his sense of the romantic is, is indicated by his concluding remark: "It must always be living. It is in the sense of living intensity, living singularity that it is the vital element in poetry. The most brilliant instance of the romantic in this sense is Mr. Eliot, who incessantly revives the past and creates the future." Presumably, Stevens means that Eliot would like to see the future imbued with certain qualities of the past. For our purposes, the important thing to note is that Stevens considers an imagination kindled by the intensity of originality romantic. It is in this general sense as well as in the more conventional sense of the word that we have briefly delineated above that Stevens considers himself romantic.

But if Stevens lauds these aspects of the romantic, and if he is self-admittedly a romantic in this sense, he is aware of the awkward position in society he occupies because of it. "Sailing after Lunch" is a poem which expresses in a comic manner the common theme of the alienation of the poet or the intellectual. The title evokes that precarious, sinking feeling familiar to modern writers since Baudelaire remarked on the immense nausea of billboards. The poet laments our society's misunderstanding the meaning and force of the romantic. Society denies it any meaning but a pejorative one. What makes things even worse is that society may be right; for in this poem the poet himself feels anything but the master of the situation.

10. *OP*, pp. 251 f.

It is the word pejorative that hurts.
My old boat goes round on a crutch
And doesn't get under way
It's the time of the year
And the time of the day

Perhaps it's the lunch that we had
Or the lunch that we should have had.
But I am, in any case,
A most inappropriate man
In a most unpropitious place.

Despite the proper weather and time of year, the poet cannot embark. It is as if his bad pharynx were a chronic condition. Socially slighted and imaginatively frustrated, he confesses his sense of alienation. What the word "pejorative" refers to becomes clear in the stanza which follows. In it, Stevens expresses his longing for the living romantic. But it is a longing qualified by what some consider the historical facts about romanticism.

Mon Dieu, hear the poet's prayer.
The romantic should be here.
The romantic should be there.
It ought to be everywhere
But the romantic must never remain,

Mon Dieu, and must never again return.

History seems to be tolling the knell for the romantic which, in its eyes, must never remain and never again return. Stevens has nothing complimentary to say about this vapid historical judgment.

This heavy historical sail
Through the mustiest blue of the lake
In a really vertiginous boat
Is wholly the vapidest fake . . . .

He challenges it by expressing his reasons for being a romantic.

It is least what one ever sees.
It is only the way one feels, to say
Where my spirit is I am,
To say the light wind worries the sail

> To say the water is swift today,
> To expunge all people and be a pupil
> Of the gorgeous wheel and so to give
> That slight transcendence to the dirty sail,
> By light, the way one feels, sharp white,
> And then rush brightly through the
>   summer air.

Observation without feeling is not enough; it is not the romantic. It is feeling which transforms the object seen into the object imagined. Metaphors like "the light wind *worries* the sail" and "the water is *swift* today" reflect not observation, but imagination. Society being antagonistic to his romantic inclinations, the poet must "expunge all people" before he can be a pupil of the gorgeous imagination. In this way he will lend some grace, some transcendence to the unwieldly, even dirty, sail of his contemporary experience. The result may be an experience of great exhilaration. Although he sees the contemporary poet's role as highly problematic, he knows that this itself is not necessarily an exceptional condition. Other bards have overcome the violence without by the violence within. As he says in a letter written not long after the composition of the poem, "There is no reason whatever why a poet, in the sense that I have in mind, should not exist now, notwithstanding the complexity of contemporary life, and so on. Have you ever stopped to think of the extraordinary existence of Milton, in his time and under the circumstances of the world as it was then?" He adds with a typical skeptical flourish, "Milton would be just as proper, so to speak, today as he was in his actual day, and perhaps today, instead of going off on a myth, he would have stuck to the facts. Poetry will always be a phenomenal thing."[11]

The idea of order resulting from the power of imaginative life, the life of poetry, is the final note of "Sailing after Lunch." It is a theme which receives fullest expression in the notable poem "The Idea of Order at Key West." The chaos of reality is there pictured as

> The meaningless plungings of water and the wind.

But the voice of poetry, of imagination, orders the chaos and gives a hitherto unperceived intensity to experience.

11. In a letter to Ronald Lane Latimer dated Dec. 10, 1935.

> It was her voice that made
> The sky acutest at its vanishing.
> She measured to the hour its solitude.
> She was the single artificer of the world
> In which she sang. And when she sang, the sea,
> Whatever self it had, became the self
> That was her song, for she was the maker.

The imaginative order of poetry is one which yields meaning and beauty; it is that violence from within that protects us from the violence without.

> Oh! Blessed rage for order, pale Ramon,[12]
> The maker's rage to order words of the sea,
> Words of the fragrant portals, dimly-starred,
> And of ourselves and of our origins,
> In ghostlier demarcations, keener sounds.

The peculiar magic of the imagination is that, through it, life's dimensions become more specific while becoming more mysterious.

But for all of Stevens' beautifully expressed faith in the creative power of the imagination, he is too aware of the elements antagonistic to it in our time not to have serious doubts about its efficacy. Those who say that he is a sentimentalist of the imagination, that he shows, for example, none of the Yeatsian doubt of the imagination, do not take into account the great self-irony which is central in his work. They do not take into account the comic projection of the poet's plight in a work like "Sailing after Lunch," and the poems like it in tone. The best expression of this self-irony is Stevens' great comic poem "The Man on the Dump." It is the best expression of Stevens' indecorous treatment of the merely sentimental imagination. Obsolete purple poetry, abstruse philosophy, the idea of absolute truth — all come in for a satiric once-over. For these are contrary to our contemporary experience, signified by a garbage heap. The man on the dump is the poet, who, in his effort to salvage something clean and

---

12. The Ramon Fernandez of this poem is, or so Stevens says, not the French literary critic. Stevens says, "I used two everyday names. As I might have expected, they turned out to be an actual name." (See *Modern Poetry*, edited by Kimon Friar and John Malcolm Brinnin, New York, Appleton-Century Crofts, p. 538). Morse says that this helps to explain such impossible names as Canon Aspirin ("Notes Toward a Supreme Fiction").

true, must encounter not only the sordid miscellany of contemporary life but the obsolete romantic rhetoric which it conceals itself behind. The poem is consequently parody as well as satire. It is a poem which is a travesty on what we are meant to consider the traditional matter of poetry. In this sense, it is an anti-poetic poem. Where the old poet would begin his lyric with the breaking of glorious day marked by radiant dawn, Stevens begins with a drooping sunset and moonrise.

> Day creeps down. The moon is creeping up.

Still, we are listening to a poet, and even though he is on the dump, he relies somewhat on the vernacular of flowers. It is a vestigial response.

> The sun is a corbeil of flowers the moon Blanche
> Places there, a bouquet. Ho-ho . . . .

The man on the dump cannot make this comparison without laughing. It is a comparison which is odorous. For the dump is largely composed of old poetic garbage, of which the vernacular of flowers is a conspicuous example. It is part of the old imagery, an imagery which, alas, still succeeds for an imaginatively stale public.

> The dump is full
> Of images. Days pass like papers from a press.
> The bouquets come here in the papers.

Instead of a poetic image such as

> Like as the waves make to the pebbled shore
> So do our moments hasten to their end

the man on the dump must write with a truth that is expressive of his experience — "Days pass like papers from a press." The phantasmagora of the dirty quotidian proceeds:

> So the sun,
> And so the moon, both come, and the janitor's poems
> Of every day, the wrapper on the can of pears,
> The cat in the paper-bag, the corset, the box
> From Esthonia: the tiger chest, for tea.

The man on the dump reduces the poetry of exhilarating eventide to:

The freshness of night has been fresh a long time.

The dawn itself is a foggy affair; you cannot see the landscape for the metaphors. The morning zephyr is as heavy as so much popularized history.

> The freshness of morning, the blowing of day, one says
> That it puffs as Cornelius Nepos[13] reads, it puffs
> More than, less than or it puffs like this or that.

The freshness of dew and morning grass is sung:

> The green smacks in the eye, the dew in the green
> Smacks like fresh water in a can, like the sea
> On a cocoanut.

Although he has little use for dew, the man on the dump must admit that the little droplets have had great imaginative appeal. Typically he sees the manifestations of this appeal in mundane things.

> how many men have copied dew
> For buttons, how many women have covered themselves
> With dew, dew dresses, stones and chains of dew, heads
> Of the floweriest flowers dewed with the dewiest dew.
> One grows to hate these things except on the dump.

The gaudiness of dewy hairdos and dresses and pearl buttons is hateful because it is obsolete, and obsolete because it is grand; but to the man on the dump it is simply another fascinating piece of garbage, one more in the pile of scintillating sundry.

It is spring and the man on the dump sends up his hymn to the flowers the season brings:

> Now, in the time of spring (azaleas, trilliums,
> Myrtle, viburnums, daffodils, blue phlox),
> Between that disgust and this, between the things
> That are on the dump (azaleas, and so on)
> And those that will be (azaleas, and so on),
> One feels the purifying change. One rejects
> The trash.

13. Nepos, the Roman historian read in intermediate Latin courses, presents glorified pictures of historic figures for popular consumption.

The poetry of flowers has become automatic and boring. It has become simply a matter of repetition — there is no new way of conceiving of flowers imaginatively, unless it is in the mock-heroic, mock-poetic manner in which the man on the dump conceives of them. They have become standard props of the dump. But despite the disgust that the bedraggled poet feels, high on a heap of trashy images, he does feel a sense of purification. It is a mysterious rite of the spring season. The trash, the romantic obsolescence, is stripped away and reality is perceived in its routine ingloriousness. It is a reality truly felt. The action is accompanied by a modest crescendo on the inglorious bassoons. The trash is rejected.

> That's the moment when the moon creeps up
> To the bubbling of bassoons. That's the time
> One looks at the elephant-colorings of tires.
> Everything is shed; and the moon comes up as the moon
> (All its images are in the dump) and you see
> As a man (not like an image of a man),
> You see the moon rise in the empty sky.

The insight into reality here is similar to that given in "The Snow Man," where man is confronted with a plain unyielding landscape, nothingness, the old misconceptions gone and the place empty. In "The Man on the Dump" as in "The Snow Man," it is the clichéd language, the stale imagination, that is shed. The moon appears as the moon, not as "mental moonlight" ("The Comedian"), or clichés of the imagination. You see as a man, not as a man might see in some tired fiction. The moon, symbol of imagination, rises in a significantly empty sky. Both poems have to do with that receptive emptiness which is the mark of Stevens' skepticism. This stripping down to things as they are, to unadorned even arrant reality, has been, one may say, the polemic intention of Stevens' poetry. And he here regards it as such.

> One sits and beats an old tin can, lard pail.
> One beats and beats for that which one believes.
> That's what one wants to get near.

Caught as the imaginative man is between the pressures of materialism and the dullness of his society on the one hand, and the false claims upon reality of the rationalists, escapists of the mind and religious orthodox on the other, the free man has recourse only to his precarious but wonderfully intuitive self. Becoming the latest freed man does not always make a man feel like an ox.

>   Could it after all
>   Be merely oneself, as superior as the ear
>   To a crow's voice?

"What one wants to get near" is the unadulterated self, which is music to one's ear, compared to the crow's voice one hears on the dump. The clutter of stale images has its apposite sound in the night-ingale. Although its voice is heard, it is not seen. It is apparently eternal and is, therefore, as in Keats, an image which evokes longings for immutable essence. Stevens' nightingale, however, sounds and acts surprisingly like a low-down crow.

>   Did the nightingale torture the ear,
>   Pack the heart and scratch the mind? And does the ear
>   Solace itself in peevish birds?

For Stevens, man no longer finds enchantment in the mystery of the nightingale, no more than he can find peace in the ideal metaphysical speculations of the philosopher or the impassioned empty utterance of the mystic.

>   Is it peace,
>   Is it a philosopher's honeymoon, one finds
>   On the dump? Is it to sit among mattresses of the dead
>   Bottles, pots, shoes and grass and murmur *aptest eve*:
>   Is it to hear the blatter of grackles and say
>   *Invisible priest*; is it to eject, to pull
>   The day to pieces and cry *stanza my stone?*

The dump is two things. In the sense that the dump is the junk of imagination it is to be transcended; but in the sense that the dump is the undeniably unsavory aspect of contemporary society, a reality which is ours for better or worse, it is something only the rational or religious escapist would evade. One rejects the trash, the clutter of imaginative garbage which is the accumulation of the philosopher on a rosy honeymoon and the religious enthusiast with a transcendental hangover. Despite the terrifying miscellany of our materialistic world, despite a cacophony peculiarly modern ("blatter of grackles" is marvelously descriptive), the sentimental romantic murmurs his irrelevancies about *"aptest eve,"* and the religious man beseeches an *"Invisible priest."* "The Man on the Dump" offers the spectacle of the irrelevant but impassioned absolute described with Stevens' most withering wit. The concluding line is the *coup de canon.*

Where was it one first heard of the truth? The the.

The conflicting myths of the the, the various beliefs in absolute truth, in *the* truth, have been instrumental in making the dump a formidable heap. These myths add to the confusion. They compound the uninspiring sundry of existence with the bizarre miscellany of sentimental imaginings. Yet the final two words are ambiguous and probably deliberately so. He rejects the absolute and is simultaneously wistful about the integrity of the particular.

It takes the uncommon intelligence, the inner violence, the intense imagination — or what Stevens likes to call the romantic — to see what is merely sentimental and archaic in the romantic. The man on the dump is, despite his surroundings, a romantic. Despite the muck about him, his perception is unsullied. Among the dung, his imagination remains pure. It is very much with this situation in mind that Stevens can answer the question, "What, then, is a romantic poet now-a-days?" in this manner: "He happens to be one who still dwells in an ivory tower, but who insists that life would be intolerable except for the fact that one has, from the top, such an exceptional view of the public dump and the advertising signs of Snider's Catsup, Ivory Soap and Chevrolet Cars; he is the hermit who dwells alone with the sun and moon, but insists on taking a rotten newspaper."[14] Stevens makes this remark about the poetry of William Carlos Williams. Stevens has the poet sit on the dump rather than above it. The romantic poet, in Stevens' view, is one who treads the uneasy line between the integrity of the imagination and the test of that integrity, the insistence upon coming to terms with reality. Whether directly on top of the dump or somewhat higher above it, the poet knows that it composes a good part of the ineluctable landscape. It is his ivory tower, his unviolated imagination, that makes the dump livable, even

14. OP, p. 256.

interesting. This ivory tower is not an escape, but a necessity; the necessary vantage point from which the dump may be seen in its true perspective. Stevens' attitude about the dump is well-expressed in the words of Robert Wolseley, a seventeenth-century English writer whom Stevens quotes on the qualities of true genius; it makes the most flatly materialistic circumstances interesting. "Robert Wolseley said: 'True genius . . . will enter into the hardest and dryest thing, enrich the most barren Soyl, and inform the meanest and most uncomely matter . . . the baser, the emptier, the obscurer, the fouler, and the less susceptible of Ornament the subject appears to be, the more is the poet's praise . . . who, as Horace says of Homer, can fetch light out of Smoak, Roses out of Dunghills, and give a kind of Life to the Inanimate. . . .' "[15]

How far Stevens' sense of the romantic is from a more elevating sense of the romantic — say, the romantic platonism of Shelley. For Shelley, the world we live in is an exasperating phantom compared to the ideal realm which he worships. Stevens settles for this exasperation, settles pleasurably on the dump. Although the reality of the dump makes a concept like "invisible priest" ridiculous for him, there is in his mind the more modest version of the idealist, the man of imagination acting in a material world. Stevens' assertion in *Adagia*, "The poet is the priest of the invisible; not the invisible priest" should be understood in this context. It is not the poet as *vates* but the poet as imaginative man that Stevens is after; just as it is not the realm of essence but the realm of existence which captivates him. *The* truth becomes a truth as belief gives way to intelligence. The man on the dump wades through a welter of clichés to a moment of light, light without sweetness. He has a view of the uncluttered sky. It is refreshingly empty. It is like a new start. His rejection of the azaleas and so on is a moment of truth. This denudation leads him to the perception of beauty, mock-poetic though this beauty is.

Stevens typically rejects hackneyed elegance in favor of honest dirt. "Anything Is Beautiful if You Say It Is" is another example. For want of any other legitimate connection Stevens champions the homey. It is a good theme for comedy. But it is a theme so close to Stevens' heart that he can make it a subject for the elegiac. The late poem, "Large Red Man Reading" is a moving tribute to the bewitching sun-

15. NA, pp. 19 f.

dry of the world. With typical perversity, Stevens shows the superiority of pots to the distant stars. The plainest reality is an object of envy to those who have chosen to live in a non-physical world. The large red man, a persona for Stevens, helps to re-create for them the intense feeling for plain reality which they have lost.

> There were ghosts that returned to earth to hear his phrases,
> As he sat there reading, aloud, the great blue tabulae.
> They were those from the wilderness of stars that had
>   expected more.
>
> There were those that returned to hear him read from
>   the poem of life,
> Of the pans above the stove, the pots on the table,
>   the tulips among them.
> They were those that would have wept to step barefoot
>   into reality,
>
> That would have wept and been happy, have shivered in
>   the frost
> And cried out to feel it again, have run fingers over leaves
> And against the most coiled thorn, have seized on what
>   was ugly . . . .

A strikingly eloquent passage of Stevens' review of Williams is one in which he shows how the poet's involvement is not merely aesthetics but life itself. What he says about Williams does indeed apply to himself: "His passion for the anti-poetic is a blood-passion and not a passion of the inkpot. The anti-poetic is his spirit's cure. He needs it as a naked man needs shelter or as an animal needs salt."[16] Salt, not sugar.

16. *OP*, p. 255.

Chapter 5: "The Ultimate Plato"

$\mathcal{I}$n the previous chapter we have spoken of reality as the social scene and the relation of this reality to the life of the imagination. The other meaning of the word "reality" in Stevens is the world of natural phenomena and what we make of them. This aspect of reality is also seen in its ambiguity, at once friendly and indifferent, exalting and painful. Stevens confronts the social and natural reality with a thorough secularism and an insistence upon the primacy of these realities as the conditions of the truth. Not that they may not be or even should not be changed by our perceptions of them. But whatever fiction we may evolve, it will be a fiction which takes these realities as its base. The evasions and distortions of natural reality help make the social reality a dull one. By exorcising these evasions, comically and otherwise, Stevens is helping to create a fiction for Oxidia.

Despite his literary love of Plato, despite his admiration of Plato's mythological figures and subtle, imaginative (and apparently fortuitous) ordering of experience in a chaotic time, despite his sympathy for another inappropriate man in an unpropitious place who desired an impossible possible philosopher's man, Stevens sees Platonism as making such an evasion. Like the religious systems he can no longer believe in, the Platonic system rests, in Stevens' view, on the assumption of an ideal world comprehended by thought which falsifies our experience. Stevens frequently undercuts Plato because of what he considers Plato's indifference to the real world, to actuality. If imagination is to act in the real world, we must soberly recognize that, in Stevens' words, "a poet . . . lives in the world of Darwin and not in the world of Plato," pursuing the life of the imagination "as it reflects in us and about us."[1] He refers to "Plato's ghost" ("Less and Less Human O Savage Spirit") in the same way that he caricatures the idea of an exalted god. Associating Plato with the fictions of perfection, he can propose, in caricature,

> A large-sculptured, platonic person, free from
>   time,
> And imagine for him the speech he cannot
>   speak.

> ("The Pure Good of Theory")

Again, in the brief prose essay, "On Poetic Truth" (*OP*) we read what appears to be Stevens' familiar judgment of Plato.

For Plato the only reality that mattered is exemplified best for us in the principles of mathematics. The aim of our lives should be to draw ourselves away as much as possible from the unsubstantial fluctuating facts of the world about us and establish some communion with the objects which are apprehended by thought and not sense. This was the source of Plato's asceticism. It must suffice here to note the dismissal of the individual and particular facts of experience as of no importance in themselves. Plato would describe himself as a realist in the sense that it is by breaking away from the world of facts that we make contact with reality.

What do we learn? Just this; that poetry has to do with reality in that concrete and individual aspect of it which the mind can never tackle altogether on its own terms, with matter that is foreign and alien in a way in which abstract systems, ideas in which we detect an inherent pattern, a structure that belongs to the ideas themselves can never be. It is never

1. "Honors and Acts," IV, *OP*, p. 246.

familiar to us in the way in which Plato wished the conquests of the mind to be familiar. On the contrary its function, the need which it meets and which has to be met in some way in every age that is not to become decadent or barbarous is precisely this contact with reality as it impinges on us from the outside, the sense that we can touch and feel a solid reality which does not wholly dissolve itself into the conceptions of our own minds.[2]

Samuel French Morse informs me, however, as Joseph N. Riddel had informed him, that this was not said by Stevens. Agreeing with the ideas of H. D. Lewis' "On Poetic Truth," Stevens recorded them in a notebook, neglecting to cite his source. As Riddel writes to Morse, "Needless to say, the OP version comes out pure Stevens even if it is verbatim Lewis."[3] The essay is used, and cited, by Stevens in "About One of Marianne Moore's Poems," in *The Necessary Angel*. Here Stevens appropriates Lewis' kindred argument to describe his own feelings about Miss Moore's poetry in particular and good poetry in general.

Stevens is perpetually making distinctions between the poetic and the philosophical, the irrational and the rational, the intuitive and the deliberative, the imaginative and the systematic, the spirit of celebration and the spirit of discovery. Stevens' *Adagia* is full of a poet's complaints against philosophy. "Poetry must be irrational" is a common enough assertion, which states the poet's mistrust of reason as opposed to the ultimately intuitive grounds of truth. Stevens can even say, "As the reason destroys, the poet must create," voicing an opposition which is, in poetry, at least as old as Wordsworth's *Prelude*. Other of the *Adagia* like "Perhaps it is of more value to infuriate philosophers than to go along with them" and "Aristotle is a skeleton" show Stevens' bias. But these complaints are common to the point of almost being commonplace. It is when Stevens assaults the Platonic position that his anti-philosophical aphorisms become more engaging. For example: "The thing seen becomes the thing unseen. The opposite is, or seems to be, impossible." This is the difference between the world as we know it and the realm of ideas, an idealism of things and an idealism of ideas. It is also the difference between symbolism and allegory. The allegorist, recognizing the primacy of the world beyond, parcels the infinite out into recognizable spiritual fragments and labels. The symbolist postulates the primacy

2. *OP*, p. 236.
3. In a letter dated Oct. 22, 1959.

of things, which are themselves sources of transcendence. The symbolist is drawn to the object the way the allegorist is drawn to the universal. Both carry the burden of a mystery. But in the symbolist, the mystery is grounded in the physical world, the objects and conditions that we know to be real in our finite lives (even though he may use allegorical trappings, as Stevens does, to help clarify the mystery). Symbolism, the second wave of romanticism, is a way in which our secular epoch expresses its sense of wonder. Yet for Stevens wonder is not synonymous with transcendental revery, as it is with, say, Mallarmé. Stevens is not so ethereal as some of the Frenchmen he liked to read. His symbolism is an affirmation of poetic truth but is antipathetic to a realm of essences or ideas. Stevens finds the unreal dependent upon the real. He writes: "The poet must get rid of the hieratic in everything that concerns him and must move constantly in the direction of the credible. He must create his unreal out of what is real." Indeed, he goes on to say in *Adagia*, "What we have called elevation and elation on the part of the poet, which he communicates to the reader, may be not so much elevation as an incandescence of the intelligence and so more than ever a triumph over the incredible." Stevens wants, above all, to be simply himself. Like the figure of youth as a virile poet, Stevens says: "*No longer do I believe that there is a mystic muse, sister of the Minotaur. I am myself a part of what is real; and it is my own speech and the strength of it, this only that I hear or ever shall.*"[4] The poet is poet of himself and his world. In being this he is denying the reality of an ideal realm, denying the reality of heaven and of the Platonic realm of ideas. Stevens says, in the same essay, "It is important to believe that the visible is the equivalent of the invisible, and once we believe it, we have destroyed the imagination, that is to say we have destroyed the false imagination, the false conception of the imagination as some incalculable *vates* within us, unhappy Rodomontade."[5]

There is no such thing as the Word, but there are words. For Stevens a word is a name for a thing, the naming of which becomes part of its reality. A word is not a name for an ideal entity. For him, "The ideal is the actual become anemic." It is a reduction not a heightening of reality. The trouble with philosophy, in his view, is that it tends to prefer the abstract to the particular, harmonious

4. NA, p. 60.
5. NA. p. 61.

conceptions to perverse actualities. Stevens has nothing good to say about idealist abstraction: "Abstraction is a part of idealism. It is in this sense that it is ugly." His position is very far from Plato indeed. How wrong is John Malcolm Brinnin's assertion that "Stevens is the banished poet storming the Republic . . . involved by nature or by the Platonic equivalent of original sin, in sensuous reality and sensuous imagination, yet burning to come to whiteness and ascetic innocence."[6] This of a poet who counts reality in all its complication, and whose feeling for the sensuousness of the natural world rises to an elegiac tone! How can one make a Shelley out of a poet who feels that the greatest poverty is not to live in a physical world? Yet even R. P. Blackmur has referred to Stevens as "a dandy and a Platonist . . . the stroke of Platonism on poetry" in his essay "Lord Tennyson's Scissors."[7] In his most recent venture on Stevens, however, Blackmur reverses himself, saying that Stevens is not a Platonist but a nominalist where Plato was a realist, a nominalist who wants to find his names realities.[8]

The problem is not clear-cut. Although he gives no credence to an ideal world, Stevens is himself an idealist in the sense that he is a realist of the imagination. The thingishness of the thing is not all we know about reality, although it is always the beginning of what we know about it. He often asserts that to be is to be perceived, that the object needs the imagination just as the imagination cannot do without the object.

> The sun is an example. What it seems
> It is and in such seeming all things are . . . .
>
> Description is revelation. It is not
> The thing described, nor false facsimile.

> ("Description without Place" I, VI)

Description is defined neither by pure fact nor by Platonic reality.

> It is an artificial thing that exists,
> In its own seeming, plainly visible,

6. John Malcolm Brinnin, "Plato, Phoebus and the Man from Hartford," *Voices*, No. 121 (Spring, 1945), 31.
7. Blackmur, *Form and Value* . . . , p. 384.
8. R. P. Blackmur, "The Substance that Prevails," *Kenyon Review*, XVII (Winter, 1955), 98.

> Yet not too closely the double of our lives,
> Intenser than any actual life could be . . . .

("Description without Place" VI)

It is the heightening power of imagination that renders a matter of fact into a matter of interest.

> The fire burns as the novel taught it how.

("The Novel")

The important events and thoughts are also instances of the power of the imagination.

> Things are as they seem to Calvin or to Anne
> Of England, to Pablo Neruda in Ceylon,
> To Neitzsche in Basel, to Lenin by a lake.

("Description without Place" III)

These fictions may no longer be true for us, when they are facts of an heroic past which seems remote.

> But the integrations of the past are like
>
> . . . .
>
> A *Museo Olimpico*, so much
> So little, our affair, which is the affair
> Of the possible: seemings that are to be
> Seemings that it is possible may be.

("Description without Place" III)

New description is new truth. This is another way of saying that men are made out of words. Things are the way they are named, the way in which they are imaginatively conceived.

> It is a world of words to the end of it,
> In which nothing solid is its solid self.
>
> As, men make themselves their speech . . . .

("Description without Place" VII)

Man imitates the description of himself, he becomes what he is imagined to be capable of being. "Things seen are things as seen" says Stevens in *Adagia*. He even carries his idealism or imaginative realism far enough to be able to think "The world is myself. Life is myself." This extreme subjectivism is countered however by many of his other thoughts. To quote a direct contradiction, Stevens has also said that "Eventually an imaginary world is entirely without interest"; and more, "The ultimate value is reality." Those who are impatient with Stevens for being inconsistent in his thought must remember that, however engaging Stevens' ideas may be, he is a poet, not a philosopher, and is as much concerned with his response to the ideas as he is concerned with the ideas themselves. In fact, as a poet, he is not concerned with the formal promulgation of philosophic ideas at all, but with poetic propositions, which is a different thing. It is the difference between thought and the representation or imitation of thought for a desired emotional effect. It is the difference between thought and the experience of thinking. Nevertheless, the reader may be justified in demanding a unity to these propositions. Stevens, aware of the logical inconsistencies in his work, answers that a poet is not to be judged for his logic but for the poetry that he creates even because of the contradictions in his logic. He has said, "Sometimes I believe most in the imagination for a long time, and then, without reasoning about it, turn to reality and believe in that and that alone. But both of these things project themselves endlessly and I want them to do just that."[9] Solipsism is a constant in Stevens. The poem becomes the world and the world becomes the poem.

The two great forces in Stevens' world are the seductive and sometimes elusive reality and the masterful though sometimes fumbling imagination. In this masculine-feminine relationship Stevens illustrates his belief that the entanglements and resolutions of what he has called — in a phrase one may consider characteristically dubious — "the spirit's sex" ("Things of August") are no less intriguing and no less necessary than the more familiar kind of intimacy. When Stevens says in the *Adagia*, "A poet looks at the world as a man looks at a woman," he is giving a figure for the metaphysical ballet that takes place perpetually in his mind. The greatest moments of this ballet are moments of union.

> Two things of opposite nature seem to depend
> On one another, as a man depends
> On a woman, day on night, the imagined

9. Heringman, p. 6. Stevens says this in a letter dated March 20, 1951.

> On the real. This is the origin of change.
> Winter and spring, cold copulars, embrace
> And forth the particulars of rapture come.
>
> ("Notes Toward a Supreme Fiction"
> It Must Change IV)

It is the interdependence between the imagination and reality that makes for the happy union. This is similar to the early Wordsworthian idea that both nature and man half create, in a fusion of reality and imagination which makes for a harmonious oneness between man and the natural world. Like Wordsworth, but with some wariness in place of Wordsworth's theopathy, Stevens is

> A lover of the meadows and the woods,
> And mountains; and of all that we behold
> From this green earth; of all the mighty world
> Of eye, and ear — both what they half create,
> And what perceive . . . .
>
> ("Tintern Abbey")

Like Wordsworth, Stevens sees reality as an agent as well as an object. The poem needs

> . . . sun's green,
> Cloud's red, earth feeling, sky that thinks . . . .
>
> From these it takes. Perhaps it gives,
> In the universal intercourse.
>
> ("The Man with the Blue Guitar" XXII)

The creative union of imagination and the natural world is the meaning of the cryptic equation in *Adagia* between the thing imagined and the imaginer.

Proposita: 1. God and the imagination are one. 2. The thing imagined is the imaginer.

The 2nd equals the thing imagined and the imaginer are one. Hence, I suppose, the imaginer is God.

If this is an idealism, Stevens would certainly not consider it Platonic idealism. The apprehension of reality does not originate from the act of imagining, an act which is as much a fact of existence as the necessary physical world. It is as far as a naturalist can go in idealism. Stevens, then, inverts the Platonic idealism making the scene we live in the matter of his search.

Stevens has said about the intention of his poetry: "My idea is that in order to carry a thing to the extreme necessary to convey it one has to stick to it . . . . Given a fixed point of view, everything adjusts itself to that point of view; and the process of adjustment is a world of flux, as it should be for a poet."[10] Although the word "fixed" hardly does justice to his development, the "thing" which Stevens wishes to convey is the relation of the imagination to reality. He has become the master of this theme, coming closer to what he feels is true about this relation. His ultimate stand is that the two are interdependent, that reality alone, in the sense of actuality, is not enough. At worst, it can be dull fact. It becomes a living thing when viewed by the imaginative man. To put it another way, his theme is the naming of reality and the difficulties encountered in naming it; this, and responding with an imaginative courage and subtlety adequate to this great theme. For at best, reality is a constant and beautiful mistress. He is concerned with the problem of how we know what is real. He does not arrive, like a philosopher, with a formal theory of knowledge which is buttressed with an impressive logic. Stevens' is a poet's epistemology based on the irreducibility and seductiveness of objects, an epistemology which is indifferent to the dominance of reason. This, I think, is the meaning of the elusive "Metaphors of a Magnifico," a poem about epistemology.

> Twenty men crossing a bridge
> Into a village
> Are twenty men crossing twenty bridges,
> Into twenty villages,
> Or one man
> Crossing a single bridge into a village.
>
> This is old song
> That will not declare itself . . . .

10. William Carlos Williams, *Kora in Hell* (Boston: Four Seas Co., 1920), p. 17. Stevens says this in a letter dated April 9.

> Twenty men crossing a bridge,
> Into a village,
> Are
> Twenty men crossing a bridge
> Into a village.
>
> That will not declare itself
> Yet is certain as meaning . . . .
>
> The boots of the men clump
> On the boards of the bridge.
> The first white wall of the village
> Rises through fruit-trees.
>
> Of what was it I was thinking?
> So the meaning escapes.
>
> The first white wall of the village . . .
> The fruit-trees . . . .

Meaning, in the sense of what we know from reasoning about things and events, is not as certain and not as interesting as the particular landscape of the experience. The thing perceived is all that will declare itself. "Meaning escapes" but sense perception does not. It survives the logical play which has to do with meaning. It is final, final for Stevens as a base on which to build imaginative complexes of the real. Though Stevens is dealing here with theory, the tone is anything but arduous. The beauties of the sensory world reveal themselves fortuitously, casually, delightfully. We are reading a poet who is to include the following in his aphorisms: "Parfait Martinique: coffee mousse, rum on top, a little cream on top of that."

"An Ordinary Evening in New Haven" is one of Stevens' skilful statements of his theme; it has the added virtue of being one of his later statements, having the thoroughness and subtlety of a long-time adventure in reality. The poem is written in the three line pentameter stanza that Stevens finds so suitable to his meditative mood. The title of the poem, in its conspicuous inconspicuousness, tells us that this sort of cerebration is carried on all the time, even in the most common places; that reality, even plain reality, is an intricate affair. It is certainly a poem which pursues the life of the imagination "as it reflects itself in us and about us." The poetry of "Ordinary Evening" is a poetry of postulates. It is very different from the poetry of *Harmonium*, which was imagistic, gaudy, perverse. He is typically in his later poems writing a poetry of thought, a poetry which, in contradistinction to his many oblique poems, is not ashamed of naked assertion. His long-time meditation has subdued the modernist violence of much of his earlier verse. His meditation typically is about the imagination and reality. Also typical is his apparent subjectivism, his impulse to say that reality is a matter of the imagination alone; that things as they are, are things as they are perceived in the mind.

> Inescapable romance, inescapable choice
> Of dreams, disillusion as the last illusion,
> Reality as a thing seen by the mind,
>
> Not that which is but that which is apprehended,
> A mirror, a lake of reflections in a room,
> A glassy ocean lying at the door,
>
> A great town hanging pendent in a shade,
> An enormous nation happy in a style,
> Everything as unreal as real can be,
>
> In the exquisite eye.
>
> ("An Ordinary Evening in New Haven" V)

His imaginative realism is here identified with the perpetual stripping away of old illusion. Stevens is a poet of disillusion, a disillusion which is his own illusion. Reality is not the property of the hierophants but of the mind (which in its ecstasy has its own kind of hierophancy, e.g., "Sunday Morning"). The illusion of the disillusioned is that things are as they appear to the conceiving mind, "everything as unreal as real can be." The eye is "inexquisite" because without imagination, it sees plain things in their inexquisiteness. There is a gap between common things and the imagination. One of Stevens' images of the man who bridges the gap is "the ephebe" or youth, who represents the newest knowledge of reality and the imaginative rendering of reality. He appears in "Notes Toward a Supreme Fiction" and is the fictive character in the essay "The Figure of the Youth as Virile Poet." Like the good poet, he does not evade the conditions of reality but transfigures them. He is the youthful rebel who avoids the old rhetoric.

> The ephebe is solitary in his walk
> He skips the journalism of subjects, seeks out
> The perquisites of sanctity, enjoys
>
> A strong mind in a weak neighborhood . . . .
>
> ("An Ordinary Evening in New Haven" XIII)

He is opposed to the too easy idealism of the sentimentalist; he would not avoid things as they are. He sees with the greatest disillusion the conditions of our being.

> It is a fresh spiritual that he defines,
> A coldness in a long, too-constant warmth,
> A thing on the side of a house, not deep in a cloud,
>
> A difficulty that we predicate;
> The difficulty of the visible
> To the nations of the clear invisible,
>
> The actual landscape with its actual horns
> Of baker and butcher blowing, as if to hear,
> Hear hard, gets at an essential integrity.
>
> ("An Ordinary Evening in New Haven" XIII)

His vision assumes the difficulty of being, even if one of the fruits of this assumption is the coldness that the mind of winter brings. To a world coddled in the "too constant warmth" of the absurdities of "the clear invisible," it is the mission of "the ephebe" to confront the complicated actual even in its most common manifestations.

The same search on perhaps a higher intellectual level is carried on by Professor Eucalyptus, rabbi of the dry commonplace.

> The dry eucalyptus seeks god in the rainy cloud.
> Professor Eucalyptus of New Haven seeks him
> In New Haven with an eye that does not look
>
> Beyond the object. He sits in this room, beside
> The window, close to the ramshackle spout in which
> The rain falls with a ramshackle sound.
>   He seeks
> God in the object itself without much choice.
>
> ("An Ordinary Evening in New Haven" XIV)

This is the professor as hero. He is the champion of the ordinary. The real irony here is that Stevens is in the camp of the scholar, the rabbi. These are words which he uses interchangeably; they are not infrequently masks for Stevens. Like the poet, they are avatars of the imagination; they bring their meditations to bear on the world about us.[11] The new rabbis maintain the following:

> . . . The search
> For reality is as momentous as
> The search for God.

("An Ordinary Evening in New Haven" XXII)

Yet they maintain it without extravagance, for it is the reality of the mundane which we must seek out.

> A scholar, in his Segmenta, left a note,
> As follows, "The Ruler of Reality,
> If more unreal than New Haven, is not
>
> A real ruler, but rules what is unreal."
> In addition, there were draftings of him, thus:
> "He is the consort of the Queen of Fact."

("An Ordinary Evening in New Haven" XXVII)

It is the relentless courtship of reality that marks the life of the imagination. Stevens has said of "An Ordinary Evening in New Haven," "here my interest is to try to get as close to the ordinary, the commonplace and the ugly as it is possible for a poet to get. It is not a question of grim reality but of plain reality. The object is of course to purge oneself of anything false."[12]

There should be little doubt left about Stevens' alleged Platonism. Still, there remains to examine Stevens' early poem, "Homunculus et la Belle Étoile" or, as the poem reveals, little man and the beautiful star of imagination. This is the poem which contains the catchy phrase "the ultimate Plato"; it is the phrase which has perhaps as much as anything else led many readers astray on the question of Stevens' Platonism. The poem is not only not Platonic, it is anti-

---

11. *Mattino Domenicale*, p. 185. Stevens says, "Frankly, the figure of the rabbi has always been an exceedingly attractive one to me because it is the figure of a man devoted in the extreme to scholarship and at the same time making some use of it for human purposes."

12. Heringman, p. 212. Stevens says this in a letter dated May 3, 1949.

philosophical. The poem makes in verse the distinction between poetic truth and philosophic truth which we have seen Stevens make in prose. It is one of the distinguished poems in Stevens' comic canon. It begins with a description of the wonderful star.

> In the sea, Biscayne, there prinks
> The young emerald, evening star,
> Good light for drunkards, poets, widows,
> And ladies soon to be married.

The star is good for all categories of people who are likely to have active imaginations. Its light is a beacon to spontaneous, free action.

> By this light the salty fishes
> Arch in the sea like tree-branches,
> Going in many directions
> Up and down.

> This light conducts
> The thoughts of drunkards, the feelings
> Of widows and trembling ladies,
> The movements of fishes.

Indeed, the light is irresistible; it may even charm the man of deep thought, the ascetic rationalist.

> How pleasant an existence it is
> That this emerald charms philosophers,
> Until they become thoughtlessly willing
> To bathe their hearts in later moonlight,

> Knowing that they can bring back thought
> In the night that is still to be silent,
> Reflecting this thing and that,
> Before they sleep!

This indulgence in the charms of the imagination may not be the best thing for scholarship.

> It is better that, as scholars,
> They should think hard in the dark cuffs
> Of voluminous cloaks,
> And shave their heads and bodies.

But while this scholarly asceticism may be best for a life of contemplation it may be that contemplation is not the way to truth. For Plato it is. For the philosopher it is. But Stevens, a scholar of the senses, knows otherwise; he has the poet's view.

> It might well be that their mistress
> Is no gaunt fugitive phantom.
> She might, after all, be a wanton,
> Abundantly beautiful, eager,
>
> Fecund,
> From whose being by starlight on sea-coast,
> The innermost good of their seeking
> Might come in the simplest of speech.

Perhaps Stevens had these lines in mind when, in "The Figure of Youth as Virile Poet," he says: "It is the *mundo* of the imagination in which the imaginative man delights and not the gaunt world of the reason. The pleasure is the pleasure of powers that create a truth that cannot be arrived at by the reason alone, a truth that the poet recognizes by sensation. The morality of the poet's radiant and productive atmosphere is the morality of the right sensation."[13] Reality may well be the reality of the poet after all, sensuous, indulgent, prodigal, delightful in union. It may very well not have to do with the rationalist's silent struggle with reality. It is contained in the brightness of evening, obvious starlight, the "good light" for imaginative people.

> It is a good light, then, for those
> That know the ultimate Plato,
> Tranquilizing with this jewel
> The torments of confusion.

The light of the imagination, the reality of poetry, is "the ultimate Plato." That is, it out-Platos Plato. Stevens writes in the essay "Imagination as Value," "the imagination lives as the mind lives. The primitivism disappears. The Platonic resolution of diversity appears. The world is no longer an object, full of other extraneous objects, but an image. In the last analysis, it is with this image of the world that we are vitally concerned."[14] This is the sense in which Stevens is "Pla-

13. NA, pp. 57 f.
14. NA, p. 151.

tonic" — "the Platonic resolution of diversity appears." The play of the mind towards coherence, order, and meaning is a value common to Plato's fiction and to Stevens'. The chaos of reality is subdued by an imaginative order, an order which renders reality more real through the necessary unreality, the necessary angel as Stevens would say, the necessary angel of earth. Poetry is the ultimate Plato because it creates an order from the intricacies of appearance. It is in this sense that it goes Plato one better: things as they are is the indispensable structure of what we later half-subjectively conceive of as the real. Also it is the imagination rather than the reason which gives us the resolution of diversity; this too makes poetry the ultimate Plato. Stevens puts it this way:

The imagination is the power that enables us to perceive the normal in the abnormal, the opposite of chaos in chaos . . . . The truth seems to be that we live in concepts of the imagination before the reason has established them. If this is true, then reason is simply the methodizer of the imagination. It may be that the imagination is a miracle of logic and that its exquisite divinations are calculations beyond analysis, as the conclusions of the reason are calculations wholly within analysis. If so, one understands perfectly the remark that 'in the service of love and imagination nothing can be too lavish, too sublime or too festive.'[15]

Hence the orgiastic description of reality as it is imaginatively perceived in "Homunculus et la Belle Étoile." The poem might be called "The Progress of Homunculus" — from little man to lover. Reality appears as "a wanton/ Abundantly beautiful, eager,/ Fecund. . . ." The comic resolution here is a celebration of gusto, a casting out of precision.

Reality often appears to the imaginative man as a lover; we may recall, from the third chapter, the description of reality as "the sensual, the pearly spouse" ("The Sense of the Sleight-of-Hand Man"), or, the reader of Stevens may recall the early poem, significantly titled, "O Florida, Venereal Soil." Stevens' eroticism about this aspect of natural reality asserts itself with much gusto in "A Dish of Peaches in Russia."

> With my whole body I taste these peaches,
> I touch them and smell them. Who speaks?
>
> I absorb them as the Angevine
> Absorbs Anjou. I see them as a lover sees,

15. NA, pp. 153 f.

As a young lover sees the first buds of spring
And as the black Spaniard plays his guitar . . . .

. . . The peaches are large and round,

Ah! and red; and they have peach fuzz, ah!
They are full of juice and the skin is soft.

Indeed, in the service of love and imagination nothing can be too lavish. By contrast, how odd a spectacle the rationalist scholars seem in their voluminous cloaks; they are a target for Stevens' jibes.

X understands Aristotle
Instinctively, not otherwise
Hey-di-ho.

Let wise men piece the world together with
      wisdom
Or poets with holy magic.
Hey-di-ho.

("Five Grotesque Pieces" II *OP*)

If man is a rational animal, he is so by instinct. What is more, his rational faculty is not of the greatest importance. As Stevens says in *Adagia*, "We never arrive intellectually. But emotionally we arrive constantly (as in poetry, happiness, high mountains, vistas)."

We have already seen the pervasive colorlessness and rigid lack of imagination that rationalism brings in society — e.g., "The Common Life." "Six Significant Landscapes" gives us a high-spirited caricature of rationalism on a personal level; lack of imagination is equated with lack of style.

Rationalists, wearing square hats,
Think, in square rooms,
Looking at the floor,
Looking at the ceiling.
They confine themselves
To right-angled triangles.
If they tried rhomboids,
Cones, waving lines, ellipses —
As, for example, the ellipse of the half moon —
Rationalists would wear sombreros.

But even worse than the dullness of rationalist philosophers is their uncertainty. In Stevens' profile in caricature, they cannot enjoy because they cannot be sure, and they cannot be sure because they arrive at the truth by thought alone. This is why, in "Homunculus," truth appears to them as a "gaunt fugitive phantom."

Stevens' love affair with the imaginative apprehension of reality receives statement in his later as well as his early poetry. The eroticism is subdued. The marriage of imaginative mind has endured. The poem is called "Final Soliloquy of the Interior Paramour." Here too the fruits of imagination are seen as "the ultimate Plato," tranquilizing the torments of confusion.

> Light the first light of evening, as in a room
> In which we rest and, for small reason, think
> The world imagined is the ultimate good.
>
> This is, therefore, the intensest rendezvous.
> It is in that thought that we collect ourselves,
> Out of all the indifferences, into one thing:
>
> Within a single thing, a single shawl
> Wrapped tightly round us, since we are poor, a
>   warmth,
> A light, a power, the miraculous influence.

The poem is constructed on the principle of the conceit. The language and atmosphere of love are employed by Stevens in a revery on the beauty and power of the imagination. The paramour meets the world imagined and it is the "intensest rendezvous," made luminous by the "highest candle." The paramour becomes "one thing" with his love in the night "in which being there together is enough." The poem is beautifully quiet and elevated. The love reaches to beatitude.

> We say God and the imagination are one.

There, is, however, a discordant element in the midst of harmony. Phrases like "since we are poor," and "Out of all the indifferences" reflect Stevens' sense of the poverty and solitude of human life. It is mainly a late theme, fully expounded in "Esthétique du Mal." Despite this disquieting note, the imagination wins a great peace here, tranquilizing with this jewel of a poem the torments of confusion.

If such peace comes from the imaginative apprehension of felt life, chaos may come with the lack of it. Stevens has always been aware of the precariousness of man's endeavor to create a meaningful order just as he has always been aware of the limitations of an order which is no longer meaningful. This awareness motivates the comedy of "The Comedian as the Letter C" and is the cause of his irreverent attitude toward the past. This awareness reaches the proportions of obsession in the comic poem "Connoisseur of Chaos." Here Stevens makes drama out of the torments of confusion, tossed as he is between the conflicting claims of various orders. To retain one's identity in this chaos of ideas it is necessary to become a connoisseur. The first thing our connoisseur objects to is the too stringent imposition of order. The first stanza begins:

> A. A violent order is disorder . . . .

An example of this kind of order is the system of beliefs which rested on the contrast between life and death, with its forced dualism of body and soul, hell and heaven.

> After all the pretty contrast of life and death
> Proves that these opposite things partake of one,
> At least that was the theory, when Bishop's
> books
> Resolved the world. We cannot go back to that.

Stevens refers to religious myth of the past with familiar, debonair condescension. The cerebrations of bishops have little to do with the facts of life.

> The squirming facts exceed the squamous mind,
> If one may say so.

This line does, I suppose, in a precious way, sound like something squirming; the sound does seem to accompany the sense. The sense itself is that the facts exceed the grasp of the bony, perhaps bloodless, theological mind. Whatever the precise meaning, a sense of superfine name-calling is clear.

Reality has a way of surviving the assaults of the violent order which is disorder.

> . . . And yet relation appears,
> A small relation expanding like a shade
> Of a cloud on sand, a shape on the side of a hill.

The new knowledge of reality takes naturalistic form, tenuous and precarious though it may seem at first. So much for the violent order which is disorder. The connoisseur adds, to the engaging opening statement of the poem:

> . . . and
> B. A great disorder is an order.

Truth or a vision of order is arrived at by a dialectic of opposites.

> If all the green of spring was blue, and it is;
> If the flowers of South Africa were bright
> On the tables of Connecticut, and they are;
> If Englishmen lived without tea in Ceylon,
>   and they do;
> And if all went on in an orderly way,
> And it does; a law of inherent opposites,
> Of essential unity, is as pleasant as port,
> As pleasant as the brush-strokes of a bough,
> An upper, particular bough in, say, Marchand.[16]

For this dialectician, no pleasure or amusing incident is irrelevant. The conundrum with which the poem begins, itself a bit of mock-philosophy, is considerably clarified by unportentous tidbits and quirks, fragments of sensory experience and taste which, Stevens expansively notes, constitute a simple profundity. The opposites which make for order are, first, green grass and blue sky or, in Stevens' mythology, the reality of spring imaginatively seen; second, the simplicity of Connecticut graced with the exoticism of actual Africa; third, the Englishman living without tea in the heart of his tea plantation, preferring one wonders what.[17] These are examples of new viable order, illustrating "a law of inherent opposites." This is the orderly way in which all things go on. It is pleasant to the connoisseur to see order come of such apparent disorder. It is pleasant to contemplate the delicate balance between imagination and reality. Still, there remains for the reader the puzzling concluding statement of the first stanza:

> . . . These
> Two things are one. (Pages of illustrations.)

16. Jean Marchand, contemporary French painter.
17. Morse informs me that Stevens had a friend in Ceylon who used to send tea to Hartford. The friend did not like tea.

They are one because order and disorder are one in the dialectic of change. Stevens has been directly or indirectly influenced by the idealism of Hegel, claims Robert Lowell.[18] I think he is right. The violent order is disorder because it violates the dialectic movement of what Hegel would call the Idea, of what Stevens would call, however lightly documented here, the relation of imagination to reality. The great disorder is an order because it illustrates, in the words of Stevens' poem, "a law of inherent opposites,/ Of essential unity." This unity is sometimes conceived by Stevens in an historical sense. Witness his energetic rejection of the old myths, and his promulgation of an antithetical fiction or a fiction which is based on this rejection.

It is with the accents of a tired Hegelian that the penultimate stanza begins.

> A. Well, an old order is a violent one.
> This proves nothing . . . Just one more truth,
>   one more
> Element in the immense disorder of truths.

Still, the law of inherent opposites, the essential unity of history, is not the basis upon which Stevens' reputation as a connoisseur of chaos rests. Much more his concern is the intricacy of now, the law of inherent opposites which makes for the exquisite apprehension of the present. This less grand dialectic is at the core of what Stevens conceives to be the essential unity of life as we live it, if we live it — the interrelation of the imagination and reality. In "Notes Toward a Supreme Fiction," Stevens states that one of the characteristics of this fiction is that it must change. This change is seen as a function of Stevens' modest dialectic, which embraces such primal, dependent opposites as man and woman, day and night, the imagined and the real. The supreme fiction must rest on the organic bases of natural life; it must include the sense of change which we are inured to and indeed come to love. It must include the common antitheses of the life cycle. We derive these antitheses, and by extension the supreme fiction, from intuition.

> Winter and spring, cold copulars, embrace
> And forth the particulars of rapture come.

18. Robert Lowell, Review of *Transport to Summer*, by Wallace Stevens, *The Nation*, CLXVI (April 5, 1947), 400.

> Music falls on the silence like a sense,
> A passion that we feel, not understand.

An apparent disorder can be an order. Like the violent order which is disorder, it is subject to the conditions of change which control our natural lives, in history and in daily reality. This, I think, is what is meant by the cryptic assertion with which the first stanza concludes, "These/ Two things are one." Two things of opposite natures, like winter and spring, the Yankee and the African, are instances of the order that disorder imposes, are instances of the pleasant surprises of change. Ironically, the only thing that troubles the connoisseur of chaos is the possibility of an order which is absolute and immutable.

> B. It is in April as I write. The wind
> Is blowing after days of constant rain.
> All this, of course, will come to summer soon.
> But suppose the disorder of truths should ever
>   come
>
> To an order, most Plantagenet, most fixed . . . .

But this thought is necessarily a passing fancy and the delightful chaos of reality reigns once more in his mind.

> A great disorder is an order. Now, A
> And B are not like statuary, posed
> For a vista in the Louvre. They are things
>   chalked
> On the sidewalk so that the pensive man may
>   see.

His propositions make no pompous claim to permanence, but are cast in a common and ephemeral mold, a message to like-minded men. In the poem Stevens has thus far assumed a modest, playful mask, or so it seems. His theme, however, is the mastery of the challenging complexity, the dreadful miscellaneousness of life. Behind the frequently assumed mask of the comically fastidious scholar is an occupation which has affinities to the heroic.

> The pensive man . . . He sees that eagle float
> For which the intricate Alps are a single nest.

Like the eagle, the pensive connoisseur and the choice spirits like him are masters of complexity; such connoisseurship gains for one an intimate if intricate home.

If Stevens is an Hegelian in some loose sense, he is an Hegelian impatient of the past and indifferent to the future. For Stevens, these are interesting insofar as they may show us the present with greater clarity. The present, in all its intricacy, may sometimes seem too formidable a thing to face. Reality may be approached with an imagination which is an evasion, an imagination which feeds on images of everything but things as they are now. Such is the plight of Lady Lowzen. The poem seems at first an old one, but the troubadour is indubitably new.

> In Hydaspia, by Howzen,
> Lived a lady, Lady Lowzen,
> For whom what is was other things.

> ("Oak Leaves Are Hands")

For this woman what is real is things as they were. She now resides in India, dreaming of her dead heritage. She is seen as a daughter of the dead.

> Mac Mort she had been, ago,
> Twelve-legged in her ancestral hells,
> Weaving and weaving many arms.

> Even now, the center of something else,
> Merely by putting hand to brow,
> Brooding on centuries like shells.

> As the acorn broods on former oaks . . . .

The once vaunted family coat of arms is reduced by Stevens to a buglike apparition. Lady Lowzen broods on the past the way one may brood on the enigmas of a seashell. She is like an acorn, a new seed in a new incarnation, but chooses to brood on her past rather than her present potentiality. The glory of the house of Mac Mort gone, she creates a new personal fiction, euphonious, archaic, grand. She is dubbed Lady Lowzen of Howzen, the blatant rhyme underscoring her blatantly ridiculous evasion of things as they are.

> So she in Hydaspia created
> Out of the movement of few words,
> Flora Lowzen invigorated

Archaic and future happenings,
In glittering seven-colored changes,
By Howzen, the chromatic Lowzen.

It is archaic and future happenings which are invigorated by the glittering name. It smacks of the turgid elegance of the past — a past the poet perversely refers to as ancestral hells — and is designed to impress a vague posterity. It is equipped for everything but life. The name of the lady is irrelevant to the naming of reality.

Just as Lady Lowzen evades reality through a fantasy of an aristocratic past, Stanley Burnshaw distorts reality through a fantasy of a proletarian future. Burnshaw, in the thirties, was a Marxist critic who reviewed Stevens' *Ideas of Order* unfavorably.[19] But as a Marxist he could hardly interpret very well the poetry of so opposite a temperament. Far less beautiful than religion, Platonism, or an aristocratic past could be, Marxism is, in Stevens' view, no less a distortion of reality; and it is much more of a distortion of imagination. For Stevens,[20] Marxism presents a parody of logic, substituting a crass perfectionism for the conditions of existence. In the section of "Owl's Clover" (OP) called *Mr. Burnshaw and the Statue*, Stevens indulges in one of his few ventures in political satire.

. . . Everything is dead
Except the future. Always everything
That is dead except what ought to be.
All things destroy themselves or are destroyed.

The monolithic materialism of Marxism as it manifests itself in communism is yet another version of Utopia and Stevens appropriately calls it a "grubby faith."[21] This is the best he can say for it. Indeed, at its worst, communism appears to Stevens as Marx gone berserk, as in his satire on the communist totalitarian state, "Life on a Battleship" *(OP)*.

The captain said,
            "The war between classes is
A preliminary, provincial phase,

19. Burnshaw, *New Masses*, pp. 41 f.
20. In a letter to Latimer dated Oct. 5, 1935, Stevens writes, "I believe in what Mr. Filene calls up-to-date capitalism."
21. NA, p. 143.

Of the war between individuals. In time,
When earth has become a paradise, it will be
A paradise full of assassins."

Marx's dialectic materialism gives way to a dialectic of terror, as the
once rosy future becomes, in time present, an inverted Utopia. There
is a distressing lack of harmony between imagination and reality here.

To name reality rightly we must confront it squarely, master its
intricacy. Believing this strongly, Stevens is expert at detecting evasions
of reality. We have seen, in the third chapter, how heaven is considered by Stevens to be another evasion. But those who think as
Stevens does in this matter are not necessarily free of evasions of their
own. "Landscape with Boat" is a poem which offers an example of
another kind of asceticism. We are confronted with

An anti-master-man, floribund ascetic.

We are confronted with a man whose outlook works against the mastery of the intricacy of reality. Like the philosophers of "Homunculus
et La Belle Étoile," he is an ascetic, he is not a devotee of the graces
of the natural. Stevens calls him a "floribund ascetic." The word "floribund" is not in the dictionary but is a colorful coinage, implying with
the wit of oxymoron, an ornate asceticism which is moribund in being
asceticism at all. At first sight, we might think him someone whom
Stevens would consider a kindred spirit.

He brushed away the thunder, then the clouds,
Then the colossal illusion of heaven. Yet still
The sky was blue.

The myth of heaven gone, there remains a sky whose blue summons
us to the imagination of other exalted fictions. But the floribund
ascetic is unaffected by this encompassing blue.

. . . He wanted imperceptible air.
He wanted to see. He wanted the eye to see
And not be touched by blue. He wanted to
    know,
A naked man who regarded himself in the glass
Of air, who looked for the world beneath the
    blue,

> Without blue, without any turquoise tint or
>   phase,
> Any azure under-side or after-color.

In his use, abstraction becomes mere abstraction because it is not based on an apprehension of reality which includes his sensations as well as his thoughts. "He wanted imperceptible air"; he wanted a reality which has no relation to the senses. He therefore wanted observation of life without the imagining of its basic experiences. His "imperceptible air" is merely "the glass of air" or a bloodless and colorless reflection of reality. He sees the natural world without having a belief to displace it. The ascetic has arrived at arid simplicity.

> The single-colored, colorless, primitive.
> It was not as if the truth lay where he thought,
> Like a phantom, in an uncreated night.

Like the ascetic philosophers of "Homunculus et la Belle Étoile," truth is for him a phantom. It is in fact non-existent, not created, and has nothing to do with the world we know. His truth, like the truth of heaven which he brushed away, is a way of escape.

> It was easier to think it lay there. If
> It was nowhere else, it was there and because
> It was nowhere else, its place had to be
>   supposed,
> Itself had to be supposed, a thing supposed
> In a place supposed, a thing that he reached
> In a place that he reached, by rejecting what
>   he saw
> And denying what he heard. He would arrive.
> He had only not to live, to walk in the dark,
> To be projected by one void into
> Another.

His asceticism consists of denying the reality of the senses. Like Lady Lowzen he thinks what is was other things. Evading the difficulty of being, he prefers to think the truth lies elsewhere. In his bloodless abstraction, he becomes a victim of an arid idealization.

> . . . as truth to be accepted, he supposed
> A truth beyond all truths.

For him the major abstraction is not one grounded in things. That is the trouble. The problem is how to think and include life. "Landscape with Boat" is a poem which shows how not to do it. As in ascetic religion, as in Platonism, there is a distortion of natural reality.

By contrast, "The Bed of Old John Zeller" is a poem which shows how to do it, how to be metaphysical by first being physical. "John Zeller" is an undercutting of Plato and a reminder to the poet that he may not be casual about living in a physical world, that he may not be casual about the primacy of things, that he may not fall back on the idea that there is a realm of truth beyond all truths, that he may not believe, with Lady Lowzen, what is was other things.

> This structure of ideas, these ghostly sequences
> Of the mind, result only in disaster. It follows,
> Casual poet, that to add your own disorder to disaster
>
> Makes more of it. It is easy to wish for another structure
> Of ideas and to say as usual that there must be
> Other ghostly sequences and, it would be, luminous
>
> Sequences, thought of among spheres in the old peak of
>   night;
> This is the habit of wishing, as if one's grandfather lay
> In one's heart and wished as he had always wished, unable
>
> To sleep in that bed for its disorder, talking of ghostly
> Sequences that would be sleep and ting-tang tossing, so that
> He might slowly forget. It is more difficult to evade
>
> The habit of wishing and to accept the structure
> Of things as the structure of ideas. It was the structure
> Of things at least that was thought of in the old peak
>   of night.

Platonism is seen by Stevens as an idealist retreat, is seen as sentimentalism. It is substituting the wish for the difficulty of being. The poet must not casually submit to this structure of ghostly sequences; he must not repeat the wish dreams of old John Zeller. Pushed to its logical extreme, this making small of the structure of things is a denial of life.

It is an asceticism shared by the protagonist of "Landscape with Boat," an asceticism which for Stevens is a kind of suicide. The floribund ascetic, missing the structure of things, misconstrues the nature of man.

> . . . He never supposed
> That he might be truth, himself, or part of it,
> That the things that he rejected might be part
> And the irregular turquoise, part, the perceptible blue
> Grown denser, part . . . .

The perceptible color stands in opposition to the "imperceptible air" which the protagonist was seeking. Color is equated with living; if life lacks color it is not life. Color is used here as elsewhere — e.g., "Disillusionment of Ten O'Clock" — in a simultaneously literal and figurative sense. The ascetic is not committed to the world of sensation "Grown denser" by the presence of imagination. He denies the mighty world of eye and ear, the give and take between man and the natural world.

> . . . the eye so touched, so played
> Upon by clouds, the ear so magnified
> By thunder, parts, and all these things together,
> Parts, and more things, parts. He never supposed
>   divine
> Things might not look divine, nor that if nothing
> Was divine then all things were, the world itself,
> And that if nothing was the truth, then all
> Things were the truth, the world itself was the truth.

By "all things" Stevens means the totality and variety of our sense impressions and the interaction of these impressions with imagination and reflection. Stevens rejects the idea of truth only as it is conceived as *a priori* and absolute, though his statement in this poem and in, say, "On the Road Home," the last poem examined in the third chapter, might lead one astray. He is neither a nihilist nor a cynic, but a man for whom the rejection of the absolute is the condition of truth. He is not opposed to the divine so long as it does not look divine; or, in the words of "Sunday Morning," divinity must rest within our-

selves. The rejection of the absolute leaves one free to assume the
grace of divine natural humanity, and of divine nature. The protagonist, a victim of "A truth beyond all truths," misses the boat.

> Had he been better able to suppose:
> He might sit on a sofa on a balcony
> Above the Mediterranean, emerald
> Becoming emeralds. He might watch the palms
> Flap green ears in the heat. He might observe
> A yellow wine and follow a steamer's track
> And say, "The thing I hum appears to be
> The rhythm of this celestial pantomime."

The title of the poem, "Landscape with Boat," underscores the fact
that it is the obvious which the floribund ascetic denies himself. The
mood of the last lines is a familiar one in Stevens, reality as a holiday,
an apt figure for the ease and beauty with which the natural world
and the human contrivances which become one with it offer themselves up to the loving observer. The scene is as close as Stevens gets
to the concept of heaven, a celestial pantomime.

The failure of the floribund ascetic is a failure of imagination. He
has failed to see the conceptual power of a landscape because he has
failed to see the landscape itself. He has failed to perceive truth because he was not himself part of that perception. The opposite of this
Stevens character is the protagonist of "The Latest Freed Man," a
man who is free because he masters reality. He starts out like the
floribund ascetic,

> Tired of the old descriptions of the world . . . .

But here the difference ends. The latest freed man is free in that he
is not confined by a truth beyond all truth. His is not the colorless sky
of the ascetic. Released from the lock of the truth, the absolute, he
is able to perceive the particular in all its color.

> The latest freed man rose at six and sat
> On the edge of his bed. He said,
>   "I suppose there is
> A doctrine to this landscape. Yet, having just
> Escaped from the truth, the morning is color and mist,

> Which is enough; the moment's rain and sea
> This moment's sun (the strong man vaguely seen),
> Overtaking the doctrine of this landscape.

The sun, symbolic of the new dispensation, is the object of the free man's faith, a faith which is uttered as a parody of a more common liturgy.

> . . . Of him
> And of his works, I am sure. He bathes in the mist
> Like a man without a doctrine. The light he gives —
> It is how he gives his light. It is how he shines,
> Rising upon the doctors in their beds
> And on their beds . . ."
>   And so the freed man said.

The wonderful thing about the sun is that it indubitably *is*. It does not have to be explained. It is a reality without the help of metaphysics, just as a man is a man without the help of a doctrine. As in the poem "The Brave Man," the wonderful sun is salvation, even as it shines on a wilderness of doctors. In the ambience of the sun, the latest freed man can shed the old descriptions of the world. His transformation from a self dependent on doctrine to a self dependent on the conditions of being is miraculous.

> It was how the sun came shining into his room:
> To be without a description of to be,
> For a moment on rising, at the edge of the bed, to be,
> To have the ant of the self changed to an ox
> With its organic boomings, to be changed
> From a doctor into an ox, before standing up,
> To know that the change and that the ox-like struggle
> Comes from the strength that is the strength of the sun,
> Whether it comes directly or from the sun.
> It was how he was free. It was how his freedom came.
> It was being without description, being an ox.

Know the sun and it will make you free; this is the doctrine of the blood. It is with this new consciousness that the world in turn achieves a reality that it never had.

It was the importance of the trees outdoors,
The freshness of the oak-leaves, not so much
That they were oak-leaves, as the way they looked.
It was everything being more real, himself

At the centre of reality, seeing it.
It was everything bulging and blazing and big in itself,
The blue of the rug, the portrait of Vidal,[22]

Qui fait fi des joliesses banales, the chairs.

Tired of the old descriptions, the latest freed man has some of his own. These are descriptions of man in contact with the natural world. They are not descriptions which prove a doctrine; they are not descriptions of the truth. Because he is at the point at which the imagination and reality may meet, man is not an ant. He is "at the centre of reality." Reality thus imaginatively perceived assumes a monumental bigness, "bulging and blazing and big in itself." Like the modern poet, the free man is in touch with sources of power.

Stevens is a poet who makes great claims for the ordinary. This stand places him in the position of being an antagonist of the past. For Stevens, the past had a fatal weakness for the grand. His attitude toward nobility is characteristic. Stevens does not discredit the idea of nobility per se, but this concept undergoes a radical revision in his view. In the essay "The Noble Rider and the Sound of Words" Stevens makes his case for nobility. It is not a nobility of the grand but a nobility of effort, the effort involved in achieving a harmony between the imagination and reality. Just because he begins this essay with a quotation from Plato, I have heard people claim that he is a Platonist; they assume that Stevens adheres to Plato's figure of the soul (a winged horse and charioteer). The truth is that Stevens assaults this grandiose fiction, just as he finds it impossible to talk about the soul. He concurs in Coleridge's comment about "Plato's dear gorgeous nonsense," adding that the figure is "merely the emblem of a mythology, the rustic memorial of a belief in the soul and in a distinction between good and evil."[23] Just as the conclusions of the old

22. Vidal, a bookseller and amateur painter, bought paintings in Paris for Stevens. Morse informs me that Stevens had a Vidal self-portrait in his home. Morse believes that the line of French is probably from a Vidal letter, since it seems to characterize his paintings.
23. NA, pp. 3 f.

conceptions about the nature of reality and the self seem irrelevant so does the language central to it. Stevens says, "The reason why this particular figure has lost its vitality is that, in it, the imagination adheres to what is unreal . . . . It (the imagination) has the strength of reality or none at all."[24] Because of the wry lessons that history has taught about the nature of the grandiose, Stevens can say in his *Adagia*, with typical perversity, "A grandiose subject is not an assurance of a grandiose effect but most likely of the opposite." The trouble with the grand, as we have seen in such poems as "Delightful Evening," "The Poetry of Sound," "The Man on the Dump," and so many others, is that it lives exclusively in the world of the imagination, evading that venerable complication which makes for the less exalted truths of our lives. The weakness of the grand is the weakness of the imaginative. An example: commenting on Verrocchio's statue of Bartolommeo Colleoni, Stevens says, "In this statue, the opposition between the imagination and reality is too favorable to the imagination."[25] The nobility of Stevens' rider, on the other hand, consists not of his magnificence nor of his grandeur but of his being wholly human. Indeed, he says, "The modern poet knows perfectly that he cannot be too noble a rider, that he cannot rise up loftily in helmet and armor on a horse of imposing bronze."[26] The imagination of nobility is a thing of the past. This is a cause for joy as well as for, perhaps, regret. Stevens, inveterately modern, finds strength in opposing the plain beauty of our time to nobility. The noble rider must side with Cervantes in this matter, Cervantes the first great practitioner of a genre which tells us more than any other about how things really are in our everyday lives. Charming as the style of the imagination may be, it is an obvious object of ridicule when it comes into rude contact with the not-so-glorious facts of contemporary reality. Stevens adds, "Don Quixote will make it imperative for [the poet] to make a choice, to come to a decision regarding the imagination and reality; and he will find that the universal interdependence exists and hence his choice and his decision must be that they are equal and inseparable."[27] But Stevens goes even further than this. In the same essay he writes, "It is hard to think of a thing more out of time than nobility.

24. *Ibid.*, p. 7.
25. *Ibid.*, p. 8.
26. *Ibid.*, pp. 23 f.
27. *Ibid.*, p. 24.

Looked at plainly it seems false and dead and ugly . . . in our present, in the presence of our reality, the past looks false and is, therefore, dead and is, therefore, ugly; and we turn away from it as from something repulsive and particularly from the characteristic that it has a way of assuming: something that was noble in its day, grandeur that was, the rhetorical once."[28] A phrase like "the rhetorical once," is the kind of compressed satiric fineness, at the expense of the past, which is one of Stevens' marked characteristics. He concludes the essay with the remark that nobility is not for us what it was for the past, saying that "nobility is a force and not the manifestations of which it is composed."[29] For the Renaissance Verrocchio was fine. For us, to quote again this assertion from *Adagia*, "A grandiose subject is not an assurance of a grand effect but most likely, of the opposite." Conversely, nobility for us has to do with down-to-earth things of a world seen in disillusionment.

Stevens approaches the past with self-admitted prejudice. He is wilfully modern. If the choice is between the mundane object and the relics of the past, Stevens always chooses the first. His comment on Marianne Moore's charming poem "The Carriage from Sweden" (the poem being the apotheosis of that mundane object) is a case in point. In that poem Miss Moore pays fine tribute to the secular spirit of Sweden, the spirit of worldliness that goes into the woodwork craftsmanship of the carriage and other objects. Stevens is very much of Miss Moore's frame of mind in this matter. His poem "The Prejudice Against the Past" defends Miss Moore's point of view from the ravishments of past thought.

> Day is the children's friend.
> It is Marianna's Swedish cart.
> It is that and a very big hat.
>
> Confined by what they see,
> Aquiline pedants treat the cart,
> As one of the relics of the heart.
>
> They treat the philosopher's hat,
> Left thoughtlessly behind,
> As one of the relics of the mind . . . .

28. *Ibid.*, p. 35.
29. *Ibid.*, pp. 35 f.

It is a question of reality and imagination, in this case the lack of interdependence between the two. Reality, the present, the natural, is distorted by the pedants who live in the past; they can only think of relics even when they see mundane things. Stevens is saying that there is a thingishness in a thing which resists its being reduced to a proposition, that there is a living quality in objects which defies deoxidation. Only the aquiline pedants find life in a world of relics. The children, on the other hand, live in the light of ordinary day. Even better, the images that are meaningful to them are created spontaneously and from within themselves.

> Of day, then, children make
> What aquiline pedants take
> For souvenirs of time, lost time,
>
> Adieux, shapes, images —
> Not, not of day, but of themselves,
> Not of perpetual time.
>
> And, therefore, aquiline pedants find
> The philosopher's hat to be part of the mind,
> The Swedish cart to be part of the heart.

The exaltation of the present at the expense of perpetual time is part of the modernist arrogance which is typical of Stevens. It is an arrogance which thrives on the debate between actual things and what we are meant to take as remote abstractions — "the mind," "the heart." These become merely sentimental, merely antiques, the way the aquiline pedants use them.

But if Stevens' work is a debate between the old and the new, it is a debate which is in one sense never over. The rejections are final, if sometimes filial, but the affirmations are perpetually in the process of being made. The dialectic of the imagination and reality is never at an end, just as the truth is never confined, never fixed. For Stevens, the end of poetry is to confect a homey elegance. The instinctive integration of imagination and reality is a process rather than the reflection of an immutable law. The elegance derived is sometimes precarious, but the process is not. Except for the occasional dejection, the process is relentless as it must be in a world in which consciousness alone can stand against the inevitable flux. Stevens is a poet who lives in the world of Darwin and in the world of Bergson and Santayana.

After the final no there comes a yes
And on that yes the future world depends.
No was the night. Yes is the present sun.
If the rejected things, the things denied,
Slid over the western cataract, yet one,
One only, one thing that was firm, even
No greater than a cricket's horn, no more
Than a thought to be rehearsed all day, a speech,
Of the self that must sustain itself on speech,
One thing remaining, infallible, would be
Enough. Ah! douce campagna of that thing!
Green in the body, out of a petty phrase,
Out of a thing believed, a thing affirmed:
The form on the pillow humming while one sleeps,
The aureole above the humming house . . . .

It can never be satisfied, the mind, never.

("The Well Dressed Man with a Beard")

*A*t the heart of Stevens, as I have tried to show, is the joy of finding a new aesthetic, an aesthetic which is humble when compared to the grandiose myths of the past. When Stevens called "The Comedian" an "anti-mythological poem" he might have been speaking for all of his poetry, which is anti-mythological in the sense of its being aloof from any of the myths which make claims for man's heroic nature, or the identity of moral perfectibility in the universe and in man. It is indifferent to Platonic perfection, to Verrocchio nobility, to Puritan intimidation. Stevens, of course, has a myth of his own to make, a plain myth of human existence, an anti-mythological myth. Rejecting essence in the sense of ontological priority, he always prefers the human, secular predicament to a grand faith. For him, as for Sartre, the human condition — the necessity to exist in the world and to act there — is essence. As one of the apostles of existence he must make arrogant assertions for humility. He finds infinite possibilities in man's admission of his finite capabilities. He sees imaginative riches in the recognition of man's essential poverty. In "The Comedian" we have seen him giving up on what he calls the mythological because it is an evasion of the difficulty of being.

> He could not be content with counterfeit,
> With masquerade of thought, with hapless words
> That must belie the racking masquerade . . . .

> ("The Comedian")

He saw the mythological as a kind of utopianism, a wishdream which he must reject.

> There is a monotonous babbling in our dreams
> That makes them our dependent heirs, the heirs
> Of dreamers buried in our sleep, and not
> The oncoming fantasies of better birth.
> The apprentice knew these dreamers.

These lines may strike us with some surprise in a poem so spirited. Yet should we not expect this comedian, like the somber funny man of popular imagination, to show his other side? The notion of "better birth," set forth with much gaiety in many comic poems, is propounded with equal irreverence in a number of Stevens' poems which are morose. Because it is the somber underside of Stevens' comic spirit, because the dark poems can be best understood as an extension of this spirit, and because they have not been understood as a central aspect of his irreverence, this seems to me the place to explore his sense of an aesthetic of evil. For, to continue along the lines of paradox, Stevens sees this better birth coming as a result of the exaltation of human pain. He sees beauty as a function of evil.

   The roots of this prevalent cast of thought in Stevens are apparent in the famous early poem "Sunday Morning."

> Death is the mother of beauty, mystical,
> Within whose burning bosom we devise
> Our earthly mothers waiting, sleeplessly.

Using the statement of deliberate paradox, Stevens says that precisely because of our sense of the finite, of limitation, of transience, we feel the especially intense appeal of the mutable yet eternal objects of our natural lives. "The Comedian" and "Sunday Morning" state the ever-important theme of the inextricability of beauty and evil. By evil Stevens means metaphysical evil, which includes the realities of death, pain, unseemliness, and the many other limitations of finite, imperfect existence. But there is also a social meaning to the word as Stevens is to use it in "Esthétique du Mal." (The French word *mal* connotes the idea of pain or disease as well as the idea of evil.) Since it is the mythical conventions of a still numerically dominant tradition which Stevens assaults, he is, in the eyes of society, an apostle of evil. Satanic in a genteel way, he rejects what society considers morally good and opposes his own good, which appears to be evil. He says, like Milton's Satan, "Evil, be thou my good." Unlike Milton's Satan, however, he is not a rebel against a divine order which is considered a fact but one which is considered a chimera. Stevens makes an aesthetic of evil because he sees human disorder in the life about him.

Human existence, in all its poverty, is the starting point of this aesthetic. Just as Stevens' poetry is an instance of a typically modern task, the labor of denudation, it is also typically modern in its relentless quest for reality, in its attempt at reconstructing a sense of order, of direction, to human effort. Stevens' tone in this effort at reconstruction is, as we have said, humble. It is the humility of someone starting anew. He writes only "Notes" toward a supreme fiction — not necessarily exhaustive notes at that. His aesthetic is admittedly "du Mal." Impressed with the manifold quality of the naturalistic order he propounds, he sees "Thirteen Ways of Looking at a Blackbird." It is as if he were challenging the whole tradition of bird lyrics with this gaudy and subtle attempt. He so often has in mind an opposition between his way and what he considers generically as the traditional. His way is more tentative, but it is never ridiculous. The very title of his brilliant first volume of verse, *Harmonium*, implies this opposition; he is announcing himself as a voice to be heard, sonorous, melodious — but different from the authoritative old organ voice. Stevens is never grandiose; despite the stateliness of much of his verse he makes clear at the outset that he is a small, sometimes playful, kind of organ voice. Whatever his stateliness, whatever his gaiety, it all stems from the modern attempt at making a modest appraisal of human life. Engaged in a labor of reconstruction he starts from scratch, making no *a priori* assumptions about the order of the universe. This is one advantage of a secular metaphysics. Stevens has the further advantage, an historical one, of living in a time when it requires no great effort of the imagination to have a vision of the poverty of human life. The poet indeed lives in the world of Darwin, not Plato. One must have a mind of winter.

We must inquire more precisely into the nature of poverty as Stevens conceives it. The moving poem called "How to Live. What to Do" is an elaboration of the mind of winter theme.[1] The title indicates the importance of the kind of questions confronted by the concern with seeing things the way they are. Typically, the poem begins with an utterance which stands in opposition to a traditional poetic invocation which has become a cliché.

> Last evening the moon rose above this rock
> Impure upon a world unpurged.

These lines implicitly challenge the poems which begin with an exalting apostrophe to the goddess of the imagination and to the hallowed earth. Far from being the lovely, the perfect Diana, the moon is "impure"; the world is not transfigured by it, but is "unpurged." Everything shares the common imperfection. Instead of a seductive landscape, there is a barren rock. (In this poem, written in 1935, the rock does not have the symbolic meaning that it has in Stevens' last volume, *The Rock*.) Even the sun is characterized by its imperfections.

> Coldly the wind fell upon them
> In many majesties of sound;
> They that had left the flame-freaked sun
> To seek a sun of fuller fire.

"The man and his companion" leave the world of experience, the world of the flame-freaked sun, for the more intense atmosphere of imagination, or the moon, "a sun of fuller fire." They are greeted, however, only by the cold wind, which has a strange majesty of its own. It is not the majesty of lunar calm.

1. In a letter to Latimer of November 15, 1935, Stevens says that he prefers this poem to all the others in *Ideas of Order*. He adds, "A most attractive idea to me is the idea that we are all the merest biological mechanisms."

> Instead there was this tufted rock
> Massively rising high and bare

The rock is no monument, it is nothing special. The scene presents two lone men and a rock. There is no mystical communion with Cynthia, her voice is not heard.

> There was neither voice nor crested image,
> No chorister, nor priest. There was
> Only the great height of the rock
> And the two of them standing still to rest.

The bulk of the rock accentuates the immovable barrenness of the landscape. Yet there is a kind of transfiguration. It is a transfiguration of the poverty of the scene. An heroic sense of disillusion, a beauty derived from the very poverty of the scene, causes a sober elevation. It is a victory for the mind of winter.

> There was the cold wind and the sound
> It made, away from the muck of the land
> That they had left, heroic sound
> Joyous and jubilant and sure.

The implicit polemic intention of this poem must be underscored. The poem is entitled "How to Live. What to Do" because it is about a new knowledge of reality, a knowledge without which it is difficult to find direction in living. The poem is an example of a new sense of landscape which Stevens would like to impress upon modern man's mind; the difficulty of being finds adequate expression in the beauty of its poverty.

There is a more explicit example of Stevens' *esthétique du mal* in the poem called "The Poems of Our Climate." It opens with a picture of a still life, carnations in a porcelain bowl. The picture is perfect in its restraint and simplicity.

> Clear water in a brilliant bowl,
> Pink and white carnations. The light
> In the room more like a snowy air,
> Reflecting snow. A newly-fallen snow
> At the end of winter when afternoons return.

But there is something that the viewer's sense of beauty resists in this scene precisely because of its aesthetic qualities of untroubled simplicity. He wants some kind of complication.

> Pink and white carnations — one desires
> So much more than that. The day itself
> Is simplified: a bowl of white,
> Cold, a cold porcelain, low and round,
> With nothing more than the carnations there.

This is a sight for his grandmother but not for him. The sight is too subdued, too tame; it lacks the necessary complication, the difficult dissonance which, in our poverty, we find beautiful. The still life conceals the struggles within ourselves. It is an evasion of reality.

> Say even that this complete simplicity
> Stripped one of all one's torments, concealed
> The evilly compounded, vital I
> And made it fresh in a world of white,
> A world of clear water, brilliant-edged,
> Still one would want more, one would need more,
> More than a world of white and snowy scents.

The world of white and snowy scents is part of the idea of traditional beauty which Stevens opposes in propounding an aesthetic of evil. It is decorative in an old-fashioned way but it has no relation to a central fact of life, "The evilly compounded, vital I." By "evilly compounded" Stevens means born out of difficulty, complexity, struggle, and pain. This is his final conception of the modern self. It has the beauty of difficulty. For this reason the still life is inadequate. It reduces winter to a genteel domestic phenomenon.

> There would still remain the never-resting mind,
> So that one would want to escape, come back
> To what had been so long composed.

One would have to escape from this escape and come back to the difficulty of being. Stevens concludes:

> The imperfect is our paradise.
> Note that, in this bitterness, delight,
> Since the imperfect is so hot in us,
> Lies in flawed words and stubborn sounds.

Man is a creature who finds beauty in imperfection and arduousness. It is our element. Just as death is the mother of beauty, difficulty is the condition of truth. Tragedy is elevating, as is the recognition of our poverty. The writing of the poem is itself something of a trial. These are truths in which our sense of beauty lies, and our sense of good.

"No Possum, No Sop, No Taters" shows a landscape which is an objective correlative to the sense of evil upon which the new sense of good must rest. Written in the midst of World War II, it is a poem of great disenchantment.

> He is not here, the old sun,
> As absent as if we were asleep.
>
> The field is frozen. The leaves are dry.
> Bad is final in this light.

The old confidence that Stevens felt in the natural cycle is gone. The stalks in the fields appear as images of broken humanity.

> In this bleak air the broken stalks
> Have arms without hands. They have trunks
>
> Without legs or, for that, without heads.
> They have heads in which a captive cry
>
> Is merely the moving of a tongue.

The nightmare landscape of war is unrelieved. The poem rises to a crescendo of black poetry.

> It is deep January. The sky is hard.
> The stalks are firmly rooted in ice.
>
> It is in this solitude, a syllable,
> Out of these gawky flitterings,
>
> Intones its single emptiness,
> The savagest hollow of winter sound.
>
> It is here, in this bad, that we reach
> The last purity of the knowledge of good.

It is the recognition of the evil aspect of existence which is the basic premise of the knowledge of good. A morality which is to be true for us must be one which confronts the blackness which our fantasies, which our realities, engender. We must deal with the conspicuous presence of evil. Stevens propounds a morality which begins by confronting the fact of evil, and his sense of beauty reflects it. If evil is to be the first admission of good, ugliness will be seen to have a special beauty.

> The crow looks rusty as he rises up.
> Bright is the malice in his eye . . . .

No lovebird he.

> One joins him there for company,
> But at a distance, in another tree.

Stevens' *esthétique du mal* concerns itself with a revaluation of our sense of beauty; it embraces the beauty of the dark, the difficult, the wry. A good instance of this last mentioned kind of beauty is given in the misunderstood poem, "The Revolutionists Stop for Orangeade." With the recognition of human poverty comes a discerning taste for the wry. The revolutionists are natural man addressing God; natural, imperfect man; natural, imperfect, exasperated man.

> Capitán profundo, capitán geloso,
> Ask us not to sing standing in the sun,
> Hairy-backed and hump-armed,
> Flat-ribbed and big-bagged.
> There is no pith in music
> Except in something false.

The revolutionists, funny looking guys, are comic in their imperfection. God is their captain, unfathomable, jealous. They sing songs of praise to him, but unwillingly. There is no pith in it. It is not really relevant to their somewhat grotesque selfhood. They ask for a song more suited to the condition of their being; they know that a "false" song will be meaningful.

> Bellissimo, pomposo,
> Sing a song of serpent-kin,
> Necks among the thousand leaves,
> Tongues around the fruit.
> Sing in clownish boots
> Strapped and buckled bright.

Amidst the echoes of nursery school and the clownish accents of sing-song trochees, the theme of the poem emerges as a variation on the Fall. The song is "false" in that it has to do with evil rather than good, with disobeying the great captain rather than with supplicating him. The human condition being what it is, it is a song which makes sense to them. It is clarifying to the revolutionists to recall the origins of their revolution. Recalling the original falseness which helps to account for the unholy attraction falseness has for them strikes the revolutionists with an essential rightness. There is a Laforguian feeling, half-funny half-horrible, for the indubitable clownishness of history; it started with a fall and we have been flopping ever since. This is one of the few cases in which Stevens finds one of the old myths usable; it is used in a sense which is the opposite of orthodox, serving here as a literary analogy to our poverty. In this poem we see that it is the imperfect, the wry, the slightly absurd, the motley, the false which is our element. This is something which we can truly sing about.

> Wear the breeches of a mask,
> Coat half-flare and half galloon;
> Wear a helmet without reason,
> Tufted, tilted, twirled, and twisted.
> Start the singing in a voice
> Rougher than a grinding shale.
>
> Hang a feather by your eye,
> Nod and look a little sly.
> This must be the vent of pity,
> Deeper than a truer ditty
> Of the real that wrenches,
> Of the quick that's wry.

Considering the absurdity, the ridiculousness, the irrationality of the human condition, our outer state should represent our inner turmoil. We should appear in ludicrous garb, styled "without reason," with accoutrements tilted and twisted. Our songs should be "rough" and our aesthetic unnerving, clownish, sly. This comedy brings forth true pity. It is the truth of falseness, of wrongness. It is deeper than the "truer ditty." It is deeper than the songs which are about perfection, a cosmic plan, nobility, and what Stevens would consider the traditional sense of truth. It is deeper than the truer ditty because it does not evade the wrenching quality, the *mal* of reality.

Yvor Winters, who perceives neither the seriousness of Stevens' intentions nor the motivation behind his various masks, rebukes Stevens — rigidly — for not having had the "courage" of Crispin and taken leave of "the art which he cannot justify."[2] Winters sees Stevens as a victim of what he calls hedonism, a poet of "emotion divorced from understanding" who can find a subject for poetry "only in new degrees of intensity and strangeness"; "and as each new degree achieved becomes familiar it is submerged in the monotone of that which is no longer new, so that the search is equally devoid of hope and significance."[3] This judgment is a misinterpretation of one of the first-rate reflective poets of our time, a poet whose meditations give rise to the most intense sort of emotion. How wrong-headed is Winters' assertion that Stevens is the victim of a philosophy "which offers the cultivation of the emotions as an end in itself," in the light not only of Stevens' poetry but of his commentary on poetry. Winters says this of a poet who indulges in a "neverending meditation" on the possible new insights into reality, a poet for whom "there is no wing like meaning" (Adagia). Far from being an end in itself, the most intense emotion in Stevens accompanies integrations of imagination and reality. Yet Winters, in a dubious coupling, classifies Stevens with Poe as one who "sought only emotional stimulation in the arts" and therefore "considered novelty, and novelty of a fairly crude kind, to be an essential of good art."[4] True, Stevens is an apostle of the new, but for very different reasons. Winters sees him cultivating the new out of some decadent necessity. Emotion-seeking, after all, leads to the dead end of trying to recapture the desired emotions in new ways, trying to preserve the intensity of the experience by cultivating its strangeness. However, Stevens creates the new as an act of faith, as an act of meaning. Reality is to be perceived anew or not at all. Surely this is what Stevens means when he says, in Adagia, "Poetry is a renovation of experience." In confusing the new with novelty, Winters does Stevens a great injustice. Although Stevens would consider, say, surrealism, mere novelty, he has great praise for the new (having, no doubt, his own poetry in mind): "Newness [not novelty] may be the highest individual value in poetry. Even in the

    2. Yvor Winters, "Wallace Stevens, or The Hedonist's Progress," In Defense of Reason (Denver: University of Denver Press, 1943), p. 443.
    3. Ibid., p. 439.
    4. Ibid., p. 438.

meretricious sense of newness a new poetry has value" (*Adagia*).
For Stevens, then, novelty is the reverse of the emotional decadence
which Winters accuses him of. It is for nothing less than a very much
needed grasp of modern reality and modern beauty that Stevens is
an apostle of the new.

Stevens' irony comes of the awareness of the limitation of his position. How can we see beauty in things which are in some sense not
beautiful — imperfections, limitations, pains, and wrongs? Of course,
it would be wrong to say that Stevens, who started writing poetry with
some of the mannerisms and tastes of the dandy, thinks of beauty
only in terms of the wry. There is the incipient lotus-eater in him. As
we have shown in previous chapters, he is a poet with a magnificent
sense of natural beauty, beautiful beauty. A poem like "Meditation
Celestial and Terrestrial" in which the vaunted mind of winter dissolves because of the inebriating influence of summer is not the exception, nor is it a contradiction of the *esthétique du mal*, but another
aspect of a poet who seeks the true and complex grounds of pleasure.
In his aesthetic of evil Stevens is making a partial statement of his
idea of the real; in so doing he is solving a perplexing aesthetic problem. What is the fascination in the malice of a crow's eye? How can
wryness be the true vent of pity?

With this in mind, it is clear that a poem like "The Revolutionists
Stop for Orangeade" is, despite its apparent frivolousness, a serious
attempt at arriving at aesthetic truth. Winters sees this poem with
his characteristic humorlessness. "Since the poet, having arrived at
the predicament to which we have traced him [Winters is still equating Stevens with Crispin], however, is not to abandon his art, there
remains only the possibility that he seek variety of experience in the
increasingly perverse or strange; that he seek it, moreover, with no
feeling of respect toward the art which serves as his only instrument
and medium. In the poem entitled *The Revolutionists Stop for
Orangeade* [Winters' italics], we are given the theory of this type of
poetry."[5] To clinch his argument Winters examines the last stanza
of the poem. We are led to the conclusion that Stevens is literally
an old sailor drunk in his boots, catching tigers in red weather.

The thing Winters misses, above all, is Stevens' irony. His moral
absolutist position forces him into misleading statements about

5. *Ibid.*, p. 444.

Stevens' irony and irony in general. He sees Stevens as one of a group of poets — Byron, Laforgue, Corbière, Eliot, Pound are the others — which he calls romantic ironist. Winters' impatience with this position leads him to the following pontifical judgment: "the romantic ironists whom I have cited write imperfectly in proportion to their irony; their attitude, which is a corruption of feeling, entails a corruption of style — that is, the irony is an admission of careless feeling, which is to say careless writing, and the stylist is weak in proportion to the grounds for his irony."[6] Romantic irony is, to be sure, an irony often directed at the ironist, stemming from a sense of traditional values lost. But if it is a wry comment on the difficulties of the modern man of feeling or the modern poet, it is often a criticism of the cultural origins of these difficulties. It is an irony directed not only at the ironist but at the reader. It is not only a torment but a weapon; it not only controls the ironist but is controlled by him. It may not occur to Winters that his position is an object of this irony; Winters should lament, not the self-destructive quality of this irony, but its effectiveness in destroying the values which he does not like to see disturbed. In reality, it is not "careless feeling," much less "careless writing," which irritates Winters, but the jarring moral and aesthetic dissonance created by bold and original minds who dare disturb the universe. For the universe has disturbed them. Stevens too seeks a "rude aesthetic." He too thinks that in "a world so falsified/ The one integrity for him, the one discovery still possible to make" is to grip more closely life's "essential prose." This is self-irony but without the irresolute quality which Winters attributes to it: "the poet ridicules himself for a kind or degree of feeling which he can neither approve nor control."[7] Stevens' irony is most effective here precisely because of his control, his double-edged control. It is like the irony of the modern sculptor, who, in his impoverished aesthetic, uses wire, bolts, and rope instead of marble, in an effort to bring us to life's essential prose, to the world that surrounds us. It is an irony of a disillusioned and sly awareness, directed mainly against a stale past, a dull bowl of clichéd carnations, empty rhetoric. It is an irony which introduces a tough aesthetic — tough-minded and tough to swallow, as we have said — the way Stevens handles it. The poems of our

6. *Ibid.*, p. 73.
7. *Ibid.*, p. 70.

climate are created from impoverished "flawed words and stubborn sounds." Stevens wants to make poetry an integral part of our lives once more. He wants it to vex us into a true sense of self-awareness. The pretty is not enough. The heroic is too much.

In the late poem "The Planet on the Table," Stevens says that his poetry achieved a vision of the natural world through the arduous medium of words, and that he is satisfied with this poetry because the world had meaning in terms of everyday experience; the planet was on the table.

> Ariel was glad he had written his poems.
> They were of a remembered time
> Or of something seen that he liked . . .
>
> It was not important that they survive.
> What mattered was that they should bear
> Some lineament or character,
>
> Some affluence, if only half-perceived,
> In the poverty of their words,
> Of the planet of which they were part.

Here, despite a sense of triumph, articulation itself is considered a form of poverty, just as poetry is considered in terms of the flux of ideas and tastes. Unlike the renaissance poet, who thought in terms of universal and eternal truth, Stevens does not claim that his poetry will "eternize." The effect of Stevens' poem is one of humble serenity.

Similarly, if he negates the idea of a special providence and teleology, he does so to make a compassionate though not flamboyant affirmation.

> How mad would he have to be to say, "He beheld
> An order and thereafter he belonged
> To it"? He beheld the order of the northern sky.
>
> But the beggar gazes on calamity
> And thereafter he belongs to it, to bread
> Hard found, and water tasting of misery.
>
> For him cold's glacial beauty is his fate.
> Without understanding, he belongs to it
> And the night, and midnight, and after, where it is.

What has he? What he has he has. But what?
It is not a question of captious repartee.
What has he that becomes his heart's strong core?

He has his poverty and nothing more.
His poverty becomes his heart's strong core . . . .

("In a Bad Time")

The beggar is not an isolated case, but suffering humanity. It is the reality of this beggar which does not allow the poet to acquiesce in the notion of a divine cosmic order, even a natural cosmic order. The beggar beholds the order of poverty and lives within its laws. The reality of other orders can be denied, but his poverty cannot be; we know his look of agony is true. Any concept of a fiction which will betray so much of humanity is inadequate to our belief.

Stevens has come a long way from his inability to see much point in the life of the ordinary man. It was one of the fashionable poses of the twenties, carried somewhat over into the thirties, to be indifferent to politics and the plight of the ordinary man. As Arthur Schlesinger in his copiously anecdotal history, *The Crisis of the Old Order*, puts it:

It was an age of art, of excess, of satire, of miracle; but who was to care about economics, when business policy seemed so infallible? Or about politics, when business power seemed so invincible? If pressed, the young writer might confess himself an anarchist, devoted to the freedom of the individual, hostile to censorship and prohibition and Babbittry; but politics — So what, Oh yeah, No, Nah. 'I decline to pollute my mind with such obscenities,' said George Jean Nathan. '. . . If all the Armenians were to be killed tomorrow and if half the Russians were to starve to death the day after, it would not matter to me in the least.' 'If I am convinced of anything,' said H. L. Mencken, 'it is that Doing Good is in bad taste.' Sending money to starving children in Europe, suggested Joseph Hergesheimer, was 'one of the least engaging ways in which money could be spent.' 'I burn with generous indignation over this world's pig-headedness and injustice,' said James Branch Cabell, 'at no time whatever.'[8]

A long depression and a second World War had led Stevens to the realization that to speak of man is to speak of all men. In the middle of the thirties Stevens wrote to a friend, "I hope I am headed left, but there are lefts and lefts, and certainly I am not headed for the ghastly left of the Masses. The rich man and the comfortable man of the

8. Arthur Schlesinger, *The Crisis of the Old Order* (Boston: Houghton Mifflin, 1957), pp. 145 f.

imagination of people like Mr. Burnshaw are not nearly so rich nor nearly so comfortable as he believes them to be."[9] We all share an historical poverty, the only response to which is a heightened social responsibility. When Stevens writes to Latimer, "I am very much afraid that what you like in my poetry is just the sort of thing that you ought not to like: say, its music or color,"[10] he may not be bending appreciably left but he is certainly bending over backwards. Stevens does venture into the world of political ideas in such attempts as "Owl's Clover" and "Life on a Battleship." More than this, his "Notes Toward a Supreme Fiction" and "Esthétique du Mal," both published during World War II, propound a fiction of common humanity, a fiction which encounters the reality of human poverty. This is why, in "Notes Toward a Supreme Fiction," Stevens invokes the image of

> ... The man
> In that old coat, those sagging pantaloons,
>
> It is of him, ephebe, to make, to confect
> The final elegance, not to console
> Nor sanctify, but plainly to propound ....

If the new order, the new fiction, is to be really new and order it must be based on a radical sympathy with basic humanity. The test of the abstraction begins with the concrete in its most indisputable manifestation — common man. This is a prospect which Stevens confronts without the aid of consolation.

*   *   *

Men in general do not create in light and warmth alone. They create in darkness and coldness. They create when they are hopeless, in the midst of antagonisms, when they are wrong, when their powers are no longer subject to their control. They create as the ministers of evil. ("Two or Three Ideas," *Opus Posthumous*).

The poem central to a discussion of Stevens' idea of evil is one of the masterpieces of his later work, "Esthétique du Mal." It begins its complicated chain of thought with a familiar paradox: evil, pain, *mal* give rise to beauty. This is not stated, but is implicit in the otherwise

9. In a letter to Latimer dated Oct. 9, 1935.
10. In a letter to Latimer dated Nov. 26, 1935.

unintelligible first canto. What the reader is given is a series of instances in which *mal* is the mother of beauty.

> He was at Naples writing letters home
> And, between his letters, reading paragraphs
> On the sublime. Vesuvius had groaned
> For a month. It was pleasant to be sitting there,
> While the sultriest fulgurations, flickering
> Cast corners in the glass. He could describe
> The terror of the sound because the sound
> Was ancient.

The protagonist is in the vicinity of Vesuvius, contemplating the strange beauty of the volcano. Listening to the volcano is "pleasant" to him. This seems to be the first paradox — that nature in its violence should give pleasure. But this aesthetic paradox is foreshadowed by the seemingly casual statement of the first lines — that he is reading paragraphs on the sublime. The sublime is the sense of beauty that comes from the affective experience of anguish, the perception of man's smallness in the face of the vast, the awareness of his fragile finiteness in the ambience of the awesome infinite.

When we find that the letters he writes describe "the terror of the sound," we see that Stevens' opening casualness is a careful one, that at the very beginning of the poem he is clear about what he wishes to convey — the sense of evil which is a living presence in human existence. The protagonist, whom we may regard as Stevens, is expert at describing the violence of the volcano's fulgurations. He recalls the description of it in his letters.

> . . . He tried to remember the phrases: pain
> Audible at noon, pain torturing itself,
> Pain killing pain on the very point of pain.

He is very discriminating and skilfully descriptive in the matter of evil. Pursuing his paradoxical course, he concludes the stanza with another example of the evil as the beautiful. It takes the form of a metaphor of pain.

> The volcano trembled in another ether
> As the body trembles at the end of life.

The normality of this experience being established, Stevens begins the next stanza with a clever juxtaposition which underscores the fact that pain is a very common occurrence.

It was almost time for lunch. Pain is human.

This is followed by further illustrations of the evil as the beautiful.

There were roses in the cool café. His book
Made sure of the most correct catastrophe.

The roses are probably more than just plain red descriptive roses; they are the flower behind which is the thorn; they are the symbol, imbedded in our Western consciousness, of the oneness, the inextricability of beauty and transience. They show how death is the mother of beauty.

The allusion to tragedy, "the most correct catastrophe," is clearly in the line of paradox that Stevens has developed. In tragic suffering, because the suffering is noble, we find beauty. When Yeats, in "Lapis Lazuli," says that Hamlet and Lear are gay, he means that because they have found themselves more truly in their suffering, the gaiety of new and final self-awareness is the feeling with which the observer remains.

These meanings of beauty exist because we bring them to life. The pain, the violence of life, would have no meaning if we did not conceive it as meaningful.

Except for us, Vesuvius might consume
In solid fire the utmost earth and know
No pain (ignoring the cocks that crow us up
To die).

When we consider that the sublime traditionally implied a God who was the cause of the magnificent vast wildness before us (say, in a Claude landscape) and compare this to our present sense of the sublime as a terrible beauty which exists because we conceive it to be so, we see that our present sense of this kind of aesthetic thrill is more terrifying for being less sublime. That is, if a deity is the cause of sublimity in nature, our aesthetic indulgence receives a sanction it does not achieve when one experiences sublimity on purely secular

grounds. Unmotivated by a wish to indulge in deist notions, one finds
violence more mysterious, vastness more terrifying. Of this Stevens
writes:

> ... This is a part of the sublime
> From which we shrink. And yet, except for us,
> The total past felt nothing when destroyed.

Although we may shrink at the idea of the burden on human consciousness which the marvels of evil impose, the evil exists as an historical reality only because of human consciousness. The first fact about
an aesthetic of evil, then, is that it exists as a function of our understanding, of our imaginative apprehension of the darker aspects of
reality.

The second canto pursues further the paradoxical aspect of the
aesthetic of evil. It may be described as being a secular statement of
the *felix culpa*, the happy fall of Christian mythology, which, though
it came of our disobedience, is responsible for all that we value most
highly as noble human qualities (e.g., knowledge).

The canto begins with a stanza which is thematically rather than
dramatically related to the stanzas which had gone before it. As in
"Sunday Morning" the drama is a drama of consciousness with little
reference to an overt temporal sequence.

> At a town in which acacias grew, he lay
> On his balcony at night. Warblings became
> Too dark, too far, too much the accents of
> Afflicted sleep, too much the syllables
> That would form themselves, in time, and communicate
> The intelligence of his despair, express
> What meditation never quite achieved.

The protagonist is experiencing a dark night of the soul, and his cries
of inner anguish are echoed in his mind by the ineffable yet tortured
warblings of night birds. In the weariness of his meditation the
sounds become confused with "the accents of/ Afflicted sleep," the
mutterings of his despairing subconscious. That the dark subconscious
should achieve an incandescence of articulation which sober meditation could not achieve is yet another example of the virtues of despair
and the great grasp of evil. Despite his dark night of the soul — no,

because of it — he sees clearly his relation to the universe. He is alien to it, or it to him.

> The moon rose up as if it had escaped
> His meditation. It evaded his mind.
> It was part of a supremacy always
> Above him. The moon was always free from him,
> As night was free from him. The shadow touched
> Or merely seemed to touch him as he spoke
> A kind of elegy he found in space . . . .

His "elegy," however, is not what we might expect. It is not about the death of man's relatedness to an external cosmos, but about the life that arises from this death.

> It is pain that is indifferent to the sky
> In spite of the yellow of the acacias, the scent
> Of them in the air still hanging heavily
> In the hoary-hanging night. It does not regard
> This freedom, this supremacy, and in
> Its own hallucination never sees
> How that which rejects it saves it in the end.

Despite the friendly acacias, man is part of a cosmos which is not his friend. This is an old theme in Stevens, stated as early as "Sunday Morning" and "Nuances on a Theme by Williams." Stevens goes on to say that pain, *mal* on earth, does not concern itself with the isolation of the moon and sky, it does not regard the non-human supremacy. In the anguish of the consciousness of pain, an anguish which reaches to hallucination, one does not perceive that the isolation of the sky, the alienation of man from a cosmic order, is the condition upon which pain becomes part of beauty. Rejected by the sky, by the promise of a cosmic plan and poetic justice, man sees pain not as an anomaly but as a norm. This is the salvation of pain: recognized as an inevitable central experience of the human condition, it becomes a part of beauty. Just as suffering is noble, pain is beautiful. These concepts are defined and have meaning only in relation to the facts of being. This is how a sense of alienation from a cosmic order can give us a sense of being more at home on earth. This is what I meant in saying that this canto was a secular version of the happy fall.

If the recognition of pain as human implies the independence of man in the universe, the idea of man as a dependent being, pitied by a god, will inhibit this recognition. The third canto is an affirmation of man's independence. It opposes the old and deific with the new and naturalistic. Written in a stanza which Stevens finds very suitable to reflective, declarative poetry, the three line iambic pentameter stanza (he uses this form through the entire "Notes Toward a Supreme Fiction"), the third canto makes explicit the vocation of the protagonist. He is a poet, a poet who sees his poetry in the ambience of evil.

> His firm stanzas hang like hives in hell
> Or what hell was, since now both heaven and hell
> Are one, and here, O terra infidel.

His poetry is reflective of the moral air of earth, a composite of good and evil. If this evil were taken as a fact and not as a punishment, we would never be intimidated by an escapist sense of good. It is the idea of deity which does not permit us to create our good out of our evil. If God does not win his argument by intimidation he does so by the subtle argument of pity. To overcome a cosmic inferiority complex man must insist on the fact that at least his poverty is his own.

> The fault lies with an over-human god,
> Who by sympathy has made himself a man
> And is not to be distinguished, when we cry
>
> Because we suffer, our oldest parent, peer
> Of the populace of the heart, the reddest lord,
> Who has gone before us in experience.
>
> If only he would not pity us so much,
> Weaken our fate, relieve us of woe both great
> And small, a constant fellow of destiny,
>
> A too, too human god, self-pity's kin
> And uncourageous genesis . . . .

The "over-human god" seems to be a generalized mythological concept, a cross between Christ and the Father image. His function is through pity to relieve us of our woes. But in relieving us of our woes he is robbing us of our courage. It is for man to transform this poverty.

If Stevens insists on poverty being the province of humanity, he does so for the greater glory of man. His blasphemy is beneficent, since it has as its source a version of the good life. Although the recognition of poverty is his theme in this poem and the many poems like it, it is precisely this recognition which is the key to the world's basic wealth. What Stevens really wants is a response to life that will not falsify its conditions. He can warn us of an "uncourageous genesis" because he has a sense of courageous genesis. Following his denunciation of the pity which makes us cowards comes one of the most beautiful passages in Stevens, a devout wish, a secular prayer, for the conception of a natural life lived in the good and evil of our inheritance.

> It seems
> As if the health of the world might be enough.
>
> It seems as if the honey of common summer
> Might be enough, as if the golden combs
> Were part of a sustenance itself enough,
>
> As if hell, so modified, had disappeared,
> As if pain, no longer satanic mimicry,
> Could be borne, as if we were sure to find our way.

Although he wishes, his wish is not a benign dream. "The health of the world" includes "pain" and the honey is simply "the honey of common summer." And if the refuge of pity is given up as a solution to human woe, so is the refuge of evil, hell. For if we accept *mal* as part of our lot, we have no supernatural pain or system of pain to rely on as the scapegoat of our difficulties. Having broken with God, we need no longer pay our respects to Satan; these are the moral polarities of the old system. Christianity finds it hard to have one without the other, as the existence of Satan explains away most of the absurdities of the godhead. In the era of secularization of spirituality, pain is not our mimicking of Satan; it is not the result of our mistakes as much as it is a part of our condition. The first step toward living within the difficult conditions of existence is understanding them.

Canto four is another cryptic variation on the theme of human poverty. The proper disillusion is marred by sentimentalism, the monotonous catalogue of flowers. Opposed to the sentimentalist is the Spaniard.[11] His ambiguous rose, like the inevitable note of poverty, symbolizes the beauty of precarious circumstance. The canto concludes with a recognition of the power of the demon of poverty.

> . . . The genius of misfortune
> Is not a sentimentalist. He is
> That evil, that evil in the self, from which
> In desperate hallow, rugged gesture, fault
> Falls out on everything: the genius of
> The mind, which is our being, wrong and wrong,
> The genius of the body, which is our world,
> Spent in the false engagements of the mind.

This surrender to darkness is Stevens' not too convincing *de profundis*. It is an attempt at the articulation of — what Stevens does not completely believe in — the surrender to misfortune. Even the mind has succumbed, spending itself in false encounters with what it truly seeks.

Although pity under these conditions may be damning, sympathy is a consolation. Sympathy is the fitting coat of poverty; its genesis is human.

> Softly let all true sympathizers come,
> Without the inventions of sorrow or the sob
> Beyond invention. Within what we permit,
> Within the actual, the warm, the near,
> So great a unity, that it is bliss,
> Ties us to those we love.

Sympathy makes it easy for us to forego the chorus of pity.

> For . . .
> These nebulous brilliancies in the smallest look
> Of the being's deepest darling, we forego
> Lament, willingly forfeit the ai-ai

Stevens welcomes the intimacy of "phrases/ Compounded of dear relation"; they "mean more/ Than clouds, benevolences, distant heads." The familiar antithesis in Stevens between the new and the old, the secular and the religious, here is seen in the opposition

11. Morse informs me that "The Spaniard of the rose" is Señor Pedro Dot, a hybridizer of roses.

between sympathy and pity. The phrases compounded of dear relation are meaningful because they are "exquisite in poverty." These relations have the attributes of faith with which we vested once the golden forms of deity. This was

> Before we were wholly human and knew ourselves.

Being wholly human refers, of course, to the evolution of consciousness and not to incarnation.

A somewhat forced attempt at displaying the imperfections of nature, *mal* in the external world, is the subject of canto six.

> The sun, in clownish yellow, but not a clown,
> Brings the day to perfection and then fails.

The sun is seen as a sort of Pagliacci, its clownish yellow belying its failure. It is forced however to call the sun's falling from its noonday height a failure, or to see the progression of the seasons as an aspect of natural imperfection. The latter is convincing in Milton's myth but not in Stevens'. When Stevens writes of the sun

> . . . He dwells
> In a consummate prime, yet still desires
> A further consummation . . .

the personification is not convincing as an illustration of universal imperfection. The rest of the canto, the least successful in the poem, pursues even more strained comparisons.

The seventh canto is a variation on the familiar paradox which underlies the aesthetic of evil: an image of beauty is derived from an image of *mal*. The image of beauty is the soldier as hero. He is not a hero of greatness but of goodness. He has lived life and has therefore lived death. The soldier is a generalized mythic hero who transcends death by facing it with courage. It is his collective presence, from generation to generation, his collective heroism, which makes death meaningless.

> How red the rose that is the soldier's wound,
> The wounds of many soldiers, the wounds of all
> The soldiers that have fallen, red in blood,
> The soldier of time grown deathless in great size . . .

> . . . his wound is good because his life was.
> No part of him was ever part of death.

The lines beginning the eighth canto are well known:

> The death of Satan was a tragedy
> For the imagination. A capital
> Negation destroyed him in his tenement
> And, with him, many blue phenomena.

If the old system is to be denied, it must be completely denied, from top to bottom. From God to Satan. The moral antithesis of absolute good and absolute evil is discarded by Stevens. With it are discarded the grand and heroic myths about God and the arch-fiend. Stevens calls Satan's demise "a tragedy for the imagination." It is a tragedy for the old imagination. It is for us no tragedy at all. His death is rather comic. Satan cannot live in a tenement — it is like Verrocchio in Hartford — so he dies in one. He may survive the shafts of God but he cannot survive the quotidian.

> It was not the end he had foreseen. He knew
> That his revenge created filial
> Revenges. And negation was eccentric.
> It had nothing of the Julian thunder-cloud;
> The assassin flash and rumble . . . He was denied.

That's all. To die without a grand gesture is very embarrassing to a devil. The least that we could have done was to kill him off in the grand manner. Yet this disconcerting fate is the fate of all phantoms. The familiar irreverent manner is evident.

> Phantoms, what have you left? What underground?
> What place in which to be is not enough
> To be? You go, poor phantoms, without place
> Like silver in the sheathing of the sight,
> As the eye closes . . . .

The phantoms flee before the spectacle of being. This is a triumph for the realist, the man in quest of reality. But Stevens is far from thinking that he has found what is absolutely and immutably real, or from thinking that such a reality exists. Indeed, he feels anxious doubt about his newly won freedom.

> How cold the vacancy
> When the phantoms are gone and the shaken realist
> First sees reality.

Although he does not doubt the validity of his negation, his affirmative choice is a matter of less certainty.

> The tragedy, however, may have begun,
> Again, in the imagination's new beginning,
> In the yes of the realist spoken because he must
> Say yes, spoken because under every no
> Lay a passion for yes that had never been broken.

This assertion of the precariousness of imaginative vision is consonant with the accent of humility which Stevens assumes in his analysis of human poverty. Although there is much energy in Stevens' dialectic, the modern dialectic which negates so that it may precariously affirm, it is not the confident energy of the absolute. In the midst of his iconoclastic reveling, Stevens panics. Since the early "Sunday Morning" he has been the describer of "ambiguous undulations"; that is, the tension stated there between the "isolation of the sky" and the "chant in orgy," between the indifference of the cosmos and the necessity for new mythology, is a constant one in Stevens. He chants what he believes against a background of cosmic isolation. In "Esthétique du Mal" the isolation becomes, more than ever, the subject of the chant.

The ninth canto is a variation on the theme of "How to Live. What to Do." The moon is considered in its isolation, stripped of its traditional friendly associations. It appears slightly ridiculous in its big, unspecial facticity. We have lost the old meanings of the moon, to supply a few of our own. We have "lost the folly of the moon" to become

> The prince of the proverbs of pure poverty.

Man's isolation allows him a royal poverty. From this isolation comes the chant or imaginative vision. Isolation without the imaginative vision is destitution. But in the good light of imagination the dialectic of isolation and chant, of poverty and poetry, works toward a happy synthesis.

Here in the west indifferent crickets chant
Through our indifferent crises. Yet we require
Another chant, an incantation, as in
Another and later genesis, music
That buffets the shapes of its possible halcyon
Against the haggardie . . . A loud, large water
Bubbles up in the night and drowns the crickets'
    sound.
It is a declaration, a primitive ecstasy,
Truth's favors sonorously exhibited.

This combination of balance and sanity with hieratic ecstasy recalls "Sunday Morning," a poem which, in many ways, "Esthétique du Mal" is an answer to.

The appearance of poverty in the life cycle is the subject of canto ten. The protagonist's selection of a wife is seen to be an affirmation not only of the physical desire to relate to the reality of the natural world but of the imaginative desire as well. There is the twofold affirmation of blood and imagination, aggrandizement of the flesh and of the spirit.

        . . . His anima liked its animal
    And liked it unsubjugated, so that home
    Was a return to birth, a being born
    Again in the savagest severity,
    Desiring fiercely, the child of a mother fierce
    In his body, fiercer in his mind, merciless
    To accomplish the truth in his intelligence.

In choosing

        the most grossly maternal, the creature
    Who most fecundly assuaged him, the softest
    Woman with a vague moustache and not the mauve
    Maman

the protagonist has chosen to make a comfortable pact with reality. The woman is identified by her womanliness rather than her worldliness. Or, we may take the woman figuratively as nature in her aspect of abundance and savagery. The intercourse then is the union of imagination and reality. This puts him very much in the natural cycle of desire and pain. If the softest woman is a literal woman she is also clearly his old paramour, the natural world. She is still enough of a wanton to make him impervious to the pain of the natural cycle. It is not that pain is evaded. It is accepted, understood.

> . . . The softest woman,
> Because she is as she was, reality,
> The gross, the fecund, proved him against the touch
> Of impersonal pain.

The protagonist accepts pain as an inextricable part of his union with reality. Reality, like all mistresses, must be indulged; and she responds with a hard but true wisdom of her own.

> Reality explained.
> It was the last nostalgia: that he
> Should understand. That he might suffer or that
> He might die was the innocence of living, if life
> Itself was innocent. To say that it was
> Disentangled him from sleek ensolacings.

Seen in this way, pain has a certain innocence, the innocence of being a true condition. This realization allows man to simplify himself, to free himself from the intricacies of solace.

The powerful eleventh canto jars us immediately. Partly because it comes after the somewhat benign, for Stevens, picture of natural life presented in the preceding canto — which itself had served to mitigate the darkness of most of the poem — and partly because it is the theme of evil played dramatically with unmuted full orchestra for the first time in the poem. The chips are down. The blasphemous declaration of faith is made.

> Life is a bitter aspic. We are not
> At the centre of a diamond. At dawn,
> The paratroopers fall and as they fall
> They mow the lawn. A vessel sinks in waves
> Of people, as big bell-billows from its bell
> Bell-bellow in the village steeple. Violets,
> Great tufts, spring up from buried houses
> Of poor, dishonest people, for whom the steeple,
> Long since, rang out farewell, farewell, farewell.

The rebellious assertion of life's disjointedness made in the opening lines is supported by the various guises of evil which follow. First, there is the grim reality of war. The kaleidoscope of *mal* presents next an image of sea disaster. Finally, there is a picture of a buried town. Even the people are "poor, dishonest," in this tableau of utter poverty. It is very much in this dark mood that Stevens says in *Adagia*, "We have made too much of life. A journal of life is rarely a journal of happiness." At the very height of this despair, however, comes his most incisive utterance. The nadir of despair elicits the zenith of articulation. This is the logic of paradox of his aesthetic of evil. "The poet makes silk dresses out of worms," says Stevens in *Adagia*, meaning of course he makes beauty out of the opposite of beauty.

> Natives of poverty, children of malheur,
> The gaiety of language is our seigneur.

This wry apostrophe might serve as a motto for much of the modernist writing of our time. Stevens, like James Joyce, confronted with the cold of interstellar space on the one hand, and the loving image of unheroic humanity on the other, transfigures the tawdriness of the contemporary scene by the gaiety of language. The tone of much of Stevens' work as well as Joyce's could be described as "jocoserious."[12] When Stevens writes in *Adagia* "Poetry is a health," Joyce would agree that sanity lies in the accurate, if shocking, naming of the old and the new. In both writers, this sanity expresses itself in anything from mannered gaudiness to frenetic limpidity, from light-hearted spoofing to somber reflection. In our poverty, in our difficult individuality, it is the brilliance of language, the joy of meaning, that serves as salvation. Alienated from the notion of a familiar god, the spontaneity of our own awareness supplies a sense of order to the chaos of contemporary experience.

"Life is the elimination of what is dead" is one of Stevens' *Adagia*. The life, the reality of these tableaus of poverty, makes the traditionally rose-colored interpretations of events seem dead by comparison.

> A man of bitter appetite despises
> A well-made scene in which paratroopers

12. James Joyce, *Ulysses* (New York: Modern Library, 1942), p. 661.

Select adieux; and he despises this:
A ship that rolls on a confected ocean,
The weather pink, the wind in motion; and this:
A steeple that tip-tops the classic sun's
Arrangements; and the violets' exhumo.

These three figures share the quality of being pretty rather than true; they therefore belie beauty for "the man of bitter appetite." The second image is particularly striking. We are a long way from the Stevens of "Sea Surface Full of Clouds"; a very long way, indeed, from the poet-tourist that some critics say is the essential Stevens.

It is impossible to reconcile the poet of "Esthétique du Mal" and the many poems like it in spirit with the image of Stevens given by the best of these critics, Lionel Abel.[13] Abel's Stevens is the poet of *Harmonium* (parts of *Harmonium*), the poet whose verbs are of "the supremely comfortable sort." In his view Stevens' "poems seem to have sprung from a personal need for consummation, being part of Wallace Stevens' good time." He sees Stevens as an "amateur in that the occasion for poetry is the moment of moral release from the obligation of work." This is well observed for some of Stevens' earlier poetry. But surely Abel is trying to fit the poet to his thesis when he claims without qualification that Stevens treats love and death with "deliberate lightness, and even a touch of frivolity." Stevens' treatment of death does not end with "The Emperor of Ice-Cream"; nor is all that he has to say about love confined to "The Comedian as the Letter C." Abel engages in the same falsification when he claims that Stevens exhibits an amateur temperament in saying that "poetry is the unofficial view of being" as if this were opposed to the official, office-hours view of being; whereas in fact Stevens was contrasting poetry with philosophy, which he calls "the official view."[14] Can we accept Abel's view of Stevens as "virile, periodic, unserious and wise"? Is Stevens' poetry, as Abel maintains, "free from efforts to vindicate his profession as an important one"? This of the poet who sees "men made out of words," who begs the poet to "fix us in his conceits," who invokes the poet's "blessed rage for order," who thinks in terms of a supreme fiction! This of a poet who has said (*Adagia*), "after

13. Lionel Abel, "In the Sacred Park," *Partisan Review*, XXV (Winter, 1958), 86-98.
14. *NA*, p. 40.

one has abandoned a belief in god, poetry is that essence which takes its place as life's redemption."

I do not mean to suggest that the Stevens who "despises" the "ship that rolls on a confected ocean" is the only Stevens. The study of a modern poet is frequently a study of the masks he seriously assumes, masks which the necessary complexity of his vision calls for. The present study attempts to capture the vision of a poet who is not exclusively a tourist, a satanist, an aesthete, a metaphysician, a clown, or a rabbi. He is a poet whose complex awareness of contemporary life embraces all of these masks without being completely defined by any one of them. A master of the snicker as well as the elegiac, Stevens succeeds as only a major poet can, in a variety of guises.

The number of poems written by Stevens as aesthetician of evil and the very high quality of many of them, including the uneven but great "Esthétique du Mal," attest to this being one of the masks which Stevens finds most true. The memorable eleventh canto could have been written only by a master of his subject. Its conclusion is the work of an epicure of evil. He refers to the condemnation of the mere prettiness that belies our true condition:

> The tongue caresses these exacerbations.
> They press it as epicure, distinguishing
> Themselves from its essential savor,
> Like hunger that feeds on its own hungriness.

His condemnation of the pretty in favor of the grim gives perhaps even a sensuous pleasure. These exacerbations are a variation of the "essential savor," instances of evil, of hunger, which become enhanced and more clear by comparison with the essential evil, the universal hunger which feeds it.

Hunger feeding on its own hungriness, pain killing pain on the very point of pain — the protagonist is steeped in the cryptic calculus of evil. His knowledge of the nuances of anguish is subtle, and it is a knowledge which can be derived only for oneself. This is an aspect of difficulty which neither the knowledge of people nor the knowledge of himself can change. The evil in the world is to be accepted as a fact beyond which knowledge can take us. It is to be accepted in a

> . . . world without knowledge,
> In which no one peers, in which the will makes no

> Demands. It accepts whatever is as true,
> Including pain, which, otherwise, is false.

That is, if pain is not conceived to be a part of the condition of man, pain is falsely conceived. It is falsely conceived as a divine punishment; pain in this sense does not exist.

> In the . . . world, then, there is no pain. Yes, but
> What lover has one in such rocks, what woman,
> However known, at the centre of the heart?

The protagonist hastens to add that the doing away with pain is merely verbal; it has been done away with as a thing external to the human condition. Reality, however, in which pain is understood rather than named, proves to be a mistress whose terms are difficult.

Throughout the whole of "Esthétique du Mal" Stevens' meditations are typically concerned with the general condition of humanity rather than an individual example. We remember his protagonists, when he has them at all, not for who they are but for the reflections they embody. Similarly, he is concerned not with individual tragedy, nor a curse upon a house, but with evil as a general fact of the human condition. He is concerned with metaphysics, not ethics, just as his strength lies in the description of conditions rather than events.

> It may be that one life is a punishment
> For another, as the son's life for the father's.
> But that concerns the secondary characters.
> It is a fragmentary tragedy
> Within the universal whole. The son
> And the father alike and equally are spent,
> Each one, by the necessity of being
> Himself, the unalterable necessity
> Of being this unalterable animal.
> This force of nature in action is the major
> Tragedy.

He sees tragedy as universal rather than individual. He sees a tragic tension in all our personal lives. This recognition simplifies. Even if it means that destiny is an enemy, we gain the advantage of having our true situation clear in our minds.

                              This is destiny unperplexed,
            The happiest enemy.

The last phrase, "happiest enemy," is the epitome of the logic of
paradox employed since the last stanza. In depriving tragedy of its
individuality, in making it part of a universal whole, the recognition
of which brings a simplicity, unity, and balance of vision, the protagonist is making tragedy the opposite of tragedy. He is making it
comedy. He is saying that in recognizing tragedy as inextricably bound
with the human condition, in recognizing the pervasiveness of *mal*,
we are making a truthful assertion of consciousness which will result
in a happy, if humble, conclusion. He is sure of a bitter-sweet reality.
This certainty is something to be celebrated as well as endured. Such
is life near Vesuvius. And is not life always near Vesuvius? the protagonist would say.[15] The thirteenth canto closes with an image of
the protagonist contemplating Vesuvius, as we have seen him do at
the beginning of the poem. His many variations on the theme of evil
have left him with an even more prepossessing calm than he had at
the beginning of his meditation.

                              And it may be
            That in his Mediterranean cloister a man,
            Reclining, eased of desire, establishes
            The visible, a zone of blue and orange
            Versicolorings, establishes a time
            To watch the fire-feinting sea and calls it good,
            The ultimate good, sure of a reality
            Of the longest meditation, the maximum,
            The assassin's scene. Evil in evil is
            Comparative. The assassin discloses himself,
            The force that destroys us is disclosed, within
            This maximum, an adventure to be endured
            With the politest helplessness. Ay-mi!
            One feels its action moving in the blood.

It is a modern combination, that of whimsy, despair, and affirmation;
it is a shield which preserves us from disintegrating under the relentless ambiguity of existence.

15. Morse confirms the fact that Stevens never went to Europe. The vividness of
Vesuvius, like the vividness of many other places in his poetry, is a tribute to an active
imagination.

The fourteenth canto strikes one at first as hardly fitting into the theme and variations pattern of "Esthétique du Mal." It deals with the inadequacy of revolutionary politics, Marxist politics in particular. When we see, however, that the objection to this politics is that it is an oversimplification of reality, a failure to perceive the ambiguous nature of reality, we see the relevance of the canto. The protagonist is spoken to by Victor Serge, the expatriate Russian commentator on Soviet affairs; in Stevens' poem he is not distinguished by his personality but exclusively by his ideas.

> Victor Serge said, "I followed his argument
> With the blank uneasiness which one might
>   feel
> In the presence of a logical lunatic."
> He said it of Konstantinov.[16] Revolution
>
> Is the affair of logical lunatics.
> The politics of emotion must appear
> To be an intellectual structure. The cause
> Creates a logic not to be distinguished
> From lunacy . . . .

Revolutionary politics contains the oversimplification of a purely intellectual structure; it overlooks "the politics of emotion," the universal reality with which the individual must cope as an individual. Revolutionary politics hardens into ideology, a system of ideas with no real relation to existence. In its logical lunacy, ideology evades the intricate chaos of life from which we make our intricate order. It does not, for example, deal with the evil in life, and in its oversimplification cannot achieve a sense of beauty. Life abstracted into logic evades the ambiguous nature of existence. Thus is lost our sense of beauty deriving from difficulty and even our more conventional sense of beauty deriving from those aspects of nature which are refreshing in their simplicity, like "the lake at Geneva."

> He would not be aware of the lake.
> He would be the lunatic of one idea
> In a world of ideas, who would have all the
>   people
> Live, work, suffer and die in that idea

16. Fedor Konstantinov, apologist for Soviet policy.

In a world of ideas. He would not be aware of
  the clouds,
Lighting the martyrs of logic with white fire.
His extreme of logic would be illogical.

The "martyrs of logic" is a reference to the Genevan logicians like
Calvin who died so that an ideology might live. Calvin is another
logical lunatic. As is the case with logical lunatics one is as unconscious of the existence of the other, as they both are of anything not
included in their logic.

"Esthétique du Mal" is a tough-minded affirmation of a theme
which in Stevens becomes an obsession, the necessity to forge one's
being in the world. It is right that the concluding canto of "Esthétique du Mal" should be, in part, a paean to the natural world. It
begins with the well-known lines:

The greatest poverty is not to live
In a physical world, to feel that one's desire
Is too difficult to tell from despair. Perhaps,
After death, the non-physical people, in
  paradise,
Itself non-physical, may, by chance observe
The green corn gleaming and experience
The minor of what we feel.

There is nothing to be envied like life on earth. Stevens is more convinced of the importance of the green corn gleaming than of the
non-physical people in paradise. He knows the object of his desire. The
implication is that if one's desire is for the non-physical paradise, it
will necessarily be impossible to distinguish it from despair. Amidst
the abstract language of the last canto the physical green corn gleaming strikes us as a miraculous presence. Although the physical world
achieves an apotheosis, Stevens hastens to add that a deification of
earth is itself not a physical thing, but just as the imagination is
wedded to reality, the metaphysical takes the physical as its object.

The adventurer
In humanity has not conceived of a race
Completely physical in a physical world.
The green corn gleams and the metaphysicals

> Lie sprawling in majors of the August heat,
> The rotund emotions, paradise unknown.
> This is the thesis scrivened in delight,
> The reverberating psalm, the right chorale.

As in the penultimate stanza of "Sunday Morning," a biblical quality to the language here lends a sanctity to Stevens' secular enterprise. Here as in "Sunday Morning" we are presented with a "paradise unknown," a paradise which is not a matter of knowledge but of power. This is the end toward which an aesthetic of evil moves: concomitant to the confession of poverty and the loss of personal relation to a rational cosmic system is the assertion of a more direct if less exalted appropriation of experience, an assertion which is marked less by certainty than by the energy which it releases. "Esthétique du Mal" dissolves itself in a coda of uncertainty. It ends in a pluralistic dissonance, the afterthought of him who denies the absolute. The senses, speech, feeling, and thought may state the riddle but they do not solve it.

> One might have thought of sight, but who could think
> Of what it sees, for all the ill it sees?
> Speech found the ear, for all the evil sound,
> But the dark italics it could not propound.
> And out of what one sees and hears and out
> Of what one feels, who could have thought to make
> So many selves, so many sensuous worlds,
> As if the air, the mid-day air, was swarming
> With the metaphysical changes that occur,
> Merely in living as and where we live.

The variety of moods expressed in the last cantos of the poem leave the reader perhaps perplexed. For Stevens, this is a desired complication. If he has succeeded in conveying the essential ambiguity of life, he has succeeded. Nothing is truer for him than the ecstasy of the natural and our blindness in not seeing it.

If this sometimes borders on a manic-depressive pattern Stevens sees it. The poem "Of Bright and Blue Birds and the Gala Sun" best expresses this awareness. This moving poem, published a few years before "Esthétique du Mal," could easily serve as an epilogue to it.

> Some things, niño, some things are like this,
> That constantly and in themselves they are gay
> And you and I are such things, O most miserable . . . .

Stevens likens the precarious happiness of man to the bright and blue
birds and the gala sun which are gay in sudden, spontaneous bursts,
half chance and half impulse.

> For a moment they are gay and are a part
> Of an element, the exactest element for us,
> In which we pronounce joy like a word of our own.

When Stevens says "the exactest element for us" he is saying that
indulgence in the felicity of natural life is the thing man was most
made for. Yet here again what is dominant is a sense of the precariousness of natural felicity — we pronounce joy as if it were a word of
our own. It is precisely the consciousness of this precariousness, and
its acceptance as the unifying tone of our lives, that makes joy possible for the later Stevens. As the poem develops, joy is seen as a
property of being rather than of knowledge. It is a property of the
cognition that comes with affective experience. It relates to our precarious being in a world rather than our conceptualizing about it.
Since the state of our being is conspicuously imperfect, joy strikes
us with the relish of surprise.

> It is there, being imperfect, and with these things
> And erudite in happiness, with nothing learned,
> That we are joyously ourselves and we think
>
> Without the labor of thought, in that element,
> And we feel, in a way apart, for a moment, as if
> There was a bright *scienza* outside of ourselves,
>
> A gaiety that is being, not merely knowing,
> The will to be and to be total in belief,
> Provoking a laughter, an agreement, by surprise.

The last stanza expresses well Stevens' faith in the experience of a
paradise unknown with which "Esthétique du Mal" concludes. We
have said that this paradise was not a matter of knowledge but of
power. It is clear that this power, which is one with the negation of

the existence-denying systems, derives from the will to be in a grand-poor paradoxical place, the world.

"Esthétique du Mal" is a study in suffering but of an existential kind. Unlike another study in suffering with which it is sometimes associated because of misleading similarity in title, Baudelaire's *Les Fleurs du Mal*, it does not begin with the perception of heaven and hell. We have seen that it begins by rejecting these concepts. Baudelaire, on the other hand, begins, or certainly ends, by rejecting the natural world and the human beings that inhabit it. Although both Stevens and Baudelaire are romantics in assaulting conventional aesthetics and morality by equating beauty with pain, Stevens is no part of the most extreme romantic revolt, the revolt against being a man itself. Baudelaire's orgies of hashish and opium, his obsession with the voyage to a paradise, his affinities with Platonism are the temperamental opposite of Stevens' desired mind of winter. Stevens' sense of regeneration begins with an image of an unexalted humanity which Baudelaire could never accept. Stevens' vision is temperate; Baudelaire's resides in the heights and depths, especially the depths. Baudelaire thinks and feels in terms of Christian virtue and vice, being much more convinced of the reality of vice. For Baudelaire nature is a reproach and natural man an impossibility. When he says evil he means theological evil, even if it is lyrically rather than systematically expressed. Stevens' sense of evil is metaphysical rather than ethical. The Christian virtues and vices are irrelevant to him as such. Where for Baudelaire the distinguishing quality of humanity is man's shock of conscience, for Stevens it is the shock of consciousness. In the eyes of Stevens, although mankind may be poor it is not degraded. The last thing Stevens would want to do is what Baudelaire does, pity mankind. In showing man in his poverty and his natural surroundings, Stevens wishes to arouse him to a sense of modest possibility which will not be trammeled by the false claims of outmoded systems. Stevens embraces what Baudelaire shrinks from with loathing, the natural and the merely human. Even the dark poetry of Stevens has a sanguine final effect and, if only in an abstract way, a sense of fraternity. As has often been suggested, there is a spiritual (though hardly a formal) connection with Whitman. Baudelaire can address his reader as "Hypocrite lecteur, — mon semblable, — mon frère!" Stevens' sense of his audience, and of himself, is far less destructive.

> Follow after, O my companion, my fellow, my self
> Sister and solace, brother and delight.

("Notes Toward a Supreme Fiction" IV)

If this recalls Whitman's expansiveness it may also recall his abstractness. It may strike the reader that too often in Stevens a person is a personification. Instead of "The major man" we may want a major man or a minor one; instead of "the figure of youth" we may wish to know a particular youth living in a particular house with a particular problem; instead of "the imagination," various imaginations; instead of "it," you; in addition to more light, more heat. Yet if Stevens lacks the most intense sort of personal emotion he finds corresponding advantages. "Poetry is not personal," he spunkily asserts in *Adagia*. With his distinct rabbinical preference for thoughtful solitude to personal surrender, Stevens establishes in his large, flaunty way a relationship of self to world, a connection between his predicament and the historical moment. What poet of our century has told us more about the condition of the well-above-average sensual man? Who has studied his imaginative life more intricately or celebrated it more eloquently? Who has so happily adjusted the possibilities of life to an increasingly diminished concept of the self?

Selected Bibliography

ABEL, LIONEL. "In the Sacred Park," *Partisan Review*, XXV (Winter 1958), 86-98.
APOLLINAIRE, GUILLAUME. *Le Bestiaire*. Paris: La Sirène, 1919.
BARRETT, WILLIAM. *Irrational Man*. New York: Doubleday, 1958.
BAUDELAIRE, CHARLES. *Oeuvres*. Paris: La Pleiade, 1931.
——. *The Mirror of Art*, edited and translated by Jonathan Mayne. New York: Doubleday Anchor Books, 1956.
——. *The Essence of Laughter and Other Essays, Journals and Letters*, edited by Peter Quennel, translated by Norman Cameron. New York: Meridian Books, 1956.
BERGSON, HENRI. "Laughter," *Comedy*, edited by Wylie Sypher. New York: Doubleday Anchor Books, 1956.
BEWLEY, MARIUS. "The Poetry of Wallace Stevens," *Partisan Review*, XVI (September 1949), 895-915.
BLACKMUR, R. P. *Form and Value in Modern Poetry*. New York: Doubleday Anchor Books, 1957.
——. "The Substance that Prevails," *Kenyon Review*, XVII (Winter 1955), 94-110.

BRINNIN, JOHN MALCOLM. "Plato, Phoebus and the Man from Hartford," *Voices*, No. 121 (Spring 1945), 30-37.

BURNSHAW, STANLEY. Review of *Ideas of Order*, by Wallace Stevens, *New Masses*, XVII (October 1, 1935), 41 f.

CHASE, RICHARD. *Walt Whitman Reconsidered*. London: Victor Gollancz Ltd., 1955.

CUNNINGHAM, J. V. "The Poetry of Wallace Stevens," *Poetry*, LXXV (December 1949), 149-165.

ELLMANN, RICHARD. "Wallace Stevens' 'Ice-Cream'," *Kenyon Review*, XIX (Winter 1957), 89-105.

FORD, C. H. "Verlaine in Hartford," *View*, I (September 1940), 1, 6.

FRANKENBERG, LLOYD. *Pleasure Dome*. Boston: Houghton Mifflin, 1949.

GREGORY, HORACE. *A History of American Poetry*. New York: Harcourt, Brace, 1942.

Harvard Advocate, Stevens Issue, CXVII (December 1940).

Harvard Advocate Anthology, edited by Donald Hall. New York: Twayne Publishers, 1950.

HERINGMAN, BERNARD. "Wallace Stevens: The Reality of Poetry," unpublished Ph.D. dissertation, Columbia University, 1955.

HOWE, IRVING. Review of *Opus Posthumous*, by Wallace Stevens, *New Republic*, CXXXVII (November 4, 1957), 16-19.

JARRELL, RANDALL. *Poetry and the Age*, New York: Vintage Books, 1955.
——. Review of *Collected Poems of Wallace Stevens*, *Yale Review*, XLIV (Spring 1955), 340-346.

KAZIN, ALFRED. *On Native Grounds*. New York: Harcourt, Brace, 1942.

KREYMBORG, ALFRED. *Troubadour*. New York: Sagamore Press, 1957.

KRISTOL, IRVING. Review of *Mark Twain and Southwestern Humor*, by Kenneth S. Lynn, *Commentary*, XXIX (February 1960), 169-171.

LAFORGUE, JULES. *Oeuvres Complètes*. Paris: Mercure de France, 1917.
——. *Selected Writings of Jules Laforgue*, edited and translated by William Jay Smith. New York: Grove Press, 1956.

LOWELL, ROBERT. Review of *Transport to Summer*, by Wallace Stevens, *The Nation*, CLXVI (April 5, 1947), 400 f.

MARTZ, LOUIS. "The World as Meditation," in *English Institute Essays*, 1957. New York: Columbia University Press, 1958.
——. "The Romance of the Precise," *Yale Poetry Review*, XI (August 1949), 13-20.

MEREDITH, GEORGE. "An Essay on Comedy," in *Comedy*, edited by Wylie Sypher. New York: Doubleday Anchor Books, 1956.

MOORE, MARIANNE. *Predilections*. New York: The Viking Press, 1955.

MORSE, SAMUEL FRENCH. "The Poetry of Wallace Stevens," unpublished Ph.D. dissertation, Boston University, 1952.
——. Personal interview, March 15, 1960.

Munson, Gorham B. "The Dandyism of Wallace Stevens," *Dial,* LXXIX (November 1925), 413-417.
O'Connor, William Van. *The Shaping Spirit: A Study of Wallace Stevens.* Chicago: Henry Regnery, 1950.
Pack, Robert. *Wallace Stevens.* New Brunswick: Rutgers University Press, 1958.
Pearce, Roy Harvey. "Wallace Stevens: The Life of the Imagination," *PMLA,* LXVI (September 1951), 561-582.
Quinn, Sister M. Bernetta. "Metamorphosis in Wallace Stevens," *Sewanee Review,* LX (Spring 1952), 230-252.
Riding, Laura, and Graves, Robert. *Modernist Poetry.* New York: Doubleday, Doran, 1928.
Rosenfeld, Paul. *Men Seen.* New York: Dial Press, 1925.
Schlesinger, Arthur. *The Crisis of the Old Order.* Boston: Houghton Mifflin, 1957.
Schwartz, Delmore. "Instructed of Much Morality," *Sewanee Review,* XIV (Summer 1946), 439-448.
———. "New Verse," *Partisan Review,* IV (February 1938), 49-52.
Shattuck, Roger. "How Poetry Got Its Teeth: Paris, 1857 and After," *Western Review,* XXIII (Winter 1959), 175-186.
Simons, Hi. "The Comedian as the Letter C," *Southern Review,* V (Winter 1940), 453-468.
———. "The Genre of Wallace Stevens," *Sewanee Review,* LIII (Autumn 1945), 566-579.
Starkie, Enid. *Baudelaire.* London: Faber and Faber, 1957.
Stevens, Wallace. *The Collected Poems of Wallace Stevens.* New York: Alfred A. Knopf, 1955.
———. *Opus Posthumous,* edited by Samuel French Morse. New York: Alfred A. Knopf, 1957.
———. *The Necessary Angel.* New York: Alfred A. Knopf, 1951.
———. *Mattino Domenicale ed altre poesie,* edited and translated by Renato Poggioli. Turino: Giulio Einaudi, 1953.
———. Reply to questionnaire of Geoffrey Grigson, *New Verse,* XI (October 1934), 215.
———. "On the Poem 'Ice-Cream' and the 'Meaning' of Poetry," *The Explicator,* VII (November 1948), 18.
Sypher, Wylie, ed. *Comedy.* New York: Doubleday Anchor Books, 1956.
———. "Connoisseur in Chaos," *Partisan Review,* XII (Winter 1946), 83-94.
Tindall, William York. *The Literary Symbol.* Bloomington: Indiana University Press, 1955.
Trinity Review, Stevens Issue, VIII (May 1954).
Watts, Harold H. "Wallace Stevens and the Rock of Summer," *Kenyon Review,* XIV (Winter 1952), 122-140.

WILLIAMS, WILLIAM CARLOS. "Wallace Stevens," *Poetry,* LXXXVII (January 1956), 234-239.
——. *Kora in Hell.* Boston: Four Seas Co., 1920.
WILSON, EDMUND. *Axel's Castle.* New York: Scribners, 1931.
WINTERS, YVOR. *In Defense of Reason.* Denver: University of Denver Press, 1943.

Index